— BARRIE RICKARDS —

Partial eclipse of the author by his first thirty-pounder! The pike weighed
31½ lb and fell to a static ledgered mackerel head at long range.

BARRIE RICKARDS

Big Pike

A & C Black · London

First published in 1986 by
A & C Black (Publishers) Limited
35 Bedford Row, London WC1R 4JH

Rickards, Barrie
  Big pike.
  1. Pike fishing
  I. Title
  799.1'753   SH691.P6
  ISBN-0-7136-5652-2

ISBN 0 7136 5652 2

Printed and bound in Great Britain by
Butler & Tanner Ltd, Frome, Somerset

Contents

Dedication

When I wrote *Fishing for Big Pike* with Ray Webb, in 1970, I said 'It is our dream that a modern generation of anglers will arrive . . .'

It is perhaps ironic that many of today's generation, displaying their considerable skills and sensitivity towards pike and pike angling, would not know of Ray Webb. He has been seriously ill and in consequence has drifted slowly away from angling. Yet his contribution to the modern pike angling scene, to those considerable skills, is incalculable. Not for him the old saws, myths, fallacies and clichés. Everything he did in piking was based upon sorting out fundamental principles. Admittedly he was eccentric, but not when it came to putting the right bait in the right place. He interpreted feeding patterns, for example, with a thoroughness never before seen. His whole approach, fresh and enthusiastic, was infectious, and some of those he infected went out and contributed a little to the task of bringing piking into the twentieth century. I hope I was one of those.

For this and many other reasons I dedicate this book to Ray Webb, not only with the past in mind, but in the hope that he'll come back to piking and join the historical procession of grand old men of the sport. Today's pike anglers owe an enormous debt to Ray Webb. I hope they recognise it and never forget it.

Foreword

Fishing for Big Pike, when first published in 1971, proved a focal point for many committed pike anglers, a book which brought together a great many isolated thoughts and introduced a number of original ideas.

Perhaps for the first time acknowledged pike experts had written in considerable detail of the sit-and-wait approach to the capture of big pike by design, an attitude which gives the angler plenty of time to work out such important matters as feeding spells, bait choice and hotspots (a new concept in 1971). The book proved an immediate success and has continued to sell for much more than a decade, proving, if proof were needed, that the consistent catching of double-figure pike (and better!) can be achieved by intention.

The authors, Barrie Rickards and Ray Webb, have subsequently achieved even greater things in their fishing careers, with Barrie catching two pike over 30 lb (one, a 32-pounder, a River Great Ouse record) and their combined totals of double-figure pike are *well* in excess of a thousand. And that makes no mention of the 7 lb tench and 20 lb carp taken in recent seasons!

Fishing for Big Pike now needs a successor and here it is. This additional work reaffirms the book's premier position in pike angling literature in much the same way that the passage of time has proven beyond doubt that theories and ideas proffered a decade ago, and more, were absolutely correct.

Martin Gay
September 1986

Preface

In 1971 Ray Webb and I wrote *Fishing for Big Pike* and in 1976 it ran to a second edition (enlarged). Sales had always been good and the critics continuously kind, even dubbing the work a modern classic. We were under no illusions about our ability: as I have said before, it happened that we were *experienced* pike anglers and our observations rang bells with the increasing numbers of similarly keen pike anglers. This book is not intended to be another *Fishing for Big Pike*, for nothing can quite replace the uncertainties in piking in the 1960s. We were, almost tangibly, coming out of the dark ages of piking and our text hit the market at exactly the right moment. There was no design for this on our part, though I do recall fervently arguing with Archie Black, the publisher, that the time for such a book was *now*.

Subsequently it became clear that a third edition would be necessary, not only to bring the book up-to-date in a technical sense, but to convey to pike anglers in general the manner in which I felt that times had changed, and were ever changing. With Ray Webb out of angling altogether by 1984 the job would fall wholly to me; and at this stage it seemed that a fundamental rewrite of the book would be better than simply editing it throughout and adding chapters, as we had done previously. So this book should be regarded as one which has its roots in *Fishing for Big Pike* but which has grown and developed with the times. And much has become simpler.

Clearly I intend retaining a fair proportion of the subject matter, thoroughly updated, such as concepts of feeding patterns and hotspots. But other sections I now deem less important and have jettisoned. In 1976, for example, we were still not certain that piking in Ireland operated on the same principles, but now I am sure it does, and have omitted a section especially related to Irish piking. We now know a

8

great deal more about the ecology of pike, about its vital rôle in fisheries; and the Pike Angler's Club of Great Britain has been running for almost a decade. These and other modern aspects are woven into the fabric of what I hope will be a thorough coverage of the subject and a complete book in every sense.

Barrie Rickards
March 18th 1986

CHAPTER ONE

Pike on the feed

I don't suppose for one moment that Ray Webb discovered feeding patterns for pike, but he certainly went a long way towards recognising their real significance for the pike angler, and we attempted in 1971, in the first edition, to present the evidence. It should be remembered that at that time few people were aware that pike fed most days and for a relatively short period of that day. Nowadays this is widely accepted and there is a much deeper understanding of the complexities of the actual feeding periods. I remember that I for one was slow to be convinced by Ray – he had a deep intuition for pike angling but did not always present the evidence in the most convincing fashion. In fact, had we read the literature carefully enough we should have seen pointers to the results of our own fishing. Thus in the 1950s, Tag Barnes wrote about fishing the Lincolnshire drains, and stated that the crack of dawn for the first hour was *the* time (he was talking about autumn into early winter). Everybody thought it was a joke! The traditional way of pike fishing was to arrive around 10 a.m. – 11 a.m.; whilst this would catch you fish in December and January, you'd miss 90% of autumn fish. There is, then, a *broad* pattern: that early morning tends to be better than later and that morning as a whole is better than afternoon. Given limited time or commitment one should always arrive early and leave early rather than the opposite.

Within the broad pattern

Later on I shall deal with the exceptions to the broad scenario, but for the moment I want to talk about detailed feeding patterns within the morning period. My own experience is that feeding takes place, mostly, for about thirty minutes to two hours. About an hour is the most common. Outside these times you can still pick up the odd fish on some days, but it is striking that if you get several runs in a day, most if not all will be in one relatively short period of time. There is, however, another proviso to consider, namely that as pike are not scattered evenly throughout a water, but are located in groups in very small areas (Chapter 11), it does help if you are fishing in one of these areas! That taken for granted, the rest of my comments in this chapter apply with a vengeance.

Here are some actual examples.

Case histories

October 1st one season found several of us fishing a fenland drain before 6 a.m., that is, before dawn. The wind was quite strong, westerly, and the weather mild and moderately overcast until late in the day when it became 'cloudy bright'. The barometer had, over a period of several days, been rising steadily. Water and air temperatures were more or less constant prior to the season opening and for some time afterwards.

As dawn came each angler could be seen relaxing in the sedges, head only visible, and most of us were employing one rod with float ledgered deadbait and another with paternostered livebait. Some were using two livebait rods, both paternostered. It is often as well to fish through the dawn period with a paternoster tackle, and when visibility improves and tactical judgments can be made more easily, free-swimming livebaits can be used. Not much happened for about two hours save the odd, rash, fenland bream rolling in the waves, but at a few minutes past eight my paternostered ¾ lb perch livebait bobbed out of sight and I was in business with a battling, leaping pike, my first of the winter season. Weighed immediately this one went 16½ lb, and whilst returning it to the water I noticed my second float slide away without so much as a bob. Yet another heart-stopping battle ensued, and just as the fish hit the net I saw Hugh Reynolds a little way down the bank struggling with a big fish. Mine weighed 15 lb exactly, and Hugh's was 17¾ lb. I hurriedly got both my tackles into action in the swim again, and in fact, hadn't long to wait before further fireworks. The sport continued non-stop until about 9.15 a.m., and by 9.30 a.m. it was all over. Even though we fished on until almost dusk only one other run was registered. The total for that spectacular 1½ hours was twelve double-figure pike of 13¾ lb; 15 lb; 18¼ lb; 17¾ lb; 12 lb; 16½ lb; 15 lb; 15¼ lb; 10½ lb; 11¾ lb; 17½ lb and 14¾ lb, totalling 178 lb.

A number of smaller fish were taken, making the total over 200 lb to four anglers. My own score was seven over 10 lb and one other of 7 lb for a total weight of more than 100 lb.

Almost every fish, and certainly all the double-figure fish, fell within the 1½-hour spell. Anglers arriving at the usual 11 a.m. or thereabouts would have thought the water devoid of pike, and would have continued to think so had they fished the water for the next three weeks.

October 3rd saw us take a similar bag of eleven double-figure pike, in addition to smaller ones, again totalling over 200 lbs. My own share was eight fish, six over 10 lb, totalling just under 100 lb. The best fish falling to a half-mackerel, on my rod, weighed 19½ lb. Once again all the fish were taken during approximately 1½ hours between 8.45 a.m. and 10.15 a.m.

Two twenty-pounders and two large double-figure fish taken by the author and Bill Chillingworth on paternostered livebaits.

This pattern continued for between three and four weeks during which time some superb fishing was experienced; some of the early morning feeding spells, usually lasting 1 – 1½ hours, were over by 8 a.m. Suddenly things changed, possibly coincident with an obscure weather change, and instead of feeding in the early morning they began activities, less spectacularly as a rule, at about 1 p.m. and finished at 3 p.m. Approximately two hours feeding, with fewer fish caught than during the early morning spells, and yet the best fish, again falling to my half-mackerel, topped 20 lb. The afternoon feeding period lasted some four or five weeks when it was followed by a change to midday feeding, coinciding with the first of the real winter weather and the deadly cold dawns.

Peter Haywood's first thirty-pounder also weighed 31½lb and fell to half a mackerel. It, too, is a record for the lake in question.

I have experienced such feeding patterns commonly, both before and since the above examples, and on a number of quite different types of water. Several general conclusions can be drawn. Firstly, such short feeding periods hold good for about four to five weeks, occasionally longer, more commonly shorter. It is quite critical, I should think on *any* water, to identify the feeding pattern within two weeks; say, six full day sessions. Otherwise the angler may miss almost all the sport.

It is simply no use the angler sticking his head in the sand, saying 'What was good enough for Grandpa is good enough for me', and insisting that big pike can be caught at irregular intervals throughout most of the daylight hours.

Exceptions to the rule

There are exceptions, of course. Over and above any feeding patterns of the kind just described, some waters are good early morning waters and some good late evening waters. I know one still water where, irrespective of whether the day has been good or bad for fishing, the odd big pike can be expected in the last hour of the day. A nearby water is equally good in the early morning from this point of view. Drastic weather changes, such as melting snow water, can send fish completely off the feed. A feeding pattern that has been identified prior to the snow water may, or may not, be maintained after settled conditions are resumed. The angler may have to start all over again.

Whilst most keen pike anglers I know seem to manage three days' fishing each week, many anglers are able to fish only one day per week. In their case the chances of identifying the feeding pattern on a particular water are much less, and it becomes quite critical for them to fish from dawn till dusk, preferably using several techniques. It is even better for several anglers to combine and compare their results and experiences.

Individual fish may also be exceptions to the rules that appear to be governing most of their brethren. I suspect it is these fish that the active and persistent spinning men pick up. The top-flight spinning man may also partake of the really active feeding spells if he is there at the right time, of course, but my own experience is that big pike are more commonly taken on dead and/or livebaits during such feeding spells. A good example occurred on one of our waters a couple of years ago. Basil Chilvers, using big plugs, had taken several good fish including a pike over 10 lb, when Bill Chillingworth and Laurie Manns moved in with livebaits. Considerably better results were achieved with the livebaits, including a good fish over 20 lb.

Early morning piking, so alien to most pike anglers it seems, is probably the rule rather than the exception, until the depths of winter are reached when midday feeding becomes more common. At the moment the drain I am fishing is going well in the last hour of the day, whereas another stretch on the same water is pretty dead after midday.

In the depths of a really cold winter it does seem that the middle of the day is generally quite good. Usually we fish from dawn till dusk and I do sometimes wonder if it really matters when they feed, though I suppose if you manage to get only half a day off work then such knowledge of local or present conditions is invaluable. With a morning spare Fred Wagstaffe once told me he would fish Hickling, and with a spare afternoon he'd probably try Horsey instead. Unless of course he had a strong feeling that he ought to try such and such a swim, or such and such a method. Usually it is impossible to understand or explain feelings like this, but it is really important to give them full rein and not to restrict yourself by too much 'logical' thought.

Those spells in winter when pike seem to be feeding between 11 a.m. and 2.30 p.m. also explain Ray's magic stove. The angler is beginning to get peckish just as the pike's stomach is rumbling too. I well remember us getting three runs simultaneously from a boat on Hornsea Mere, just as Ray had got the chips and onions frying nicely. Ray got hold of his rod, John Neville refused to put out the stove because *he* had a run, and I was at the other end of the punt with a run as well. We could have gone up in smoke on that occasion had not Ray, realising that two maniacs were in the boat with him, put down his own rod and attended to the stove. Apart from the chaos, I only remember losing my fish in the reeds. I hope John lost his as well.

There was a winter a few years ago when every blasted Christmas cracker contained little plastic trumpets. Quite why these finished up in the tackle bags I'll never know, but suffice it to say that with 12 noon coming up and still no runs registered, four or five of us would line up on top of the bank and blow those trumpets for all we were worth. More often than not we had a run within half an hour. Talk about the walls of Jericho! Of course, if you behaved like that today you'd be thrown off the water.

Summer patterns

Moving on to summer fishing, there is still a really good case to be made for early morning fishing between dawn and breakfast time. Since the last hour of the day can also be pretty good it suggests that light is a factor to be taken into account. Carlton Towers in the West Riding of Yorkshire used to be a good 'last hour' water in summer and I can remember taking a fair number of fish in the 4 – 6 lb bracket, usually getting one run per session at this time. I also saw a local man take a fish of 18 lb on a float-ledgered dead mouse that he had found on the bank; this fish also took in the last minutes of daylight as I was tench fishing the next swim.

Generally, in summer the pike are more spread out and may not be bunched up into packs; their feeding habits become, probably in consequence, more individual. I have long felt that this is a contributory reason for the success of artificial lures in summer. (In winter, artificials are very much less effective.) This, and the fact that pike feed more often in summer than in winter, and heavier weed growth affords them some protection from livebaits and static deadbaits.

Most creatures, especially predators, become active around dawn and at dusk, so the behaviour of pike in general is not unusual. It just took us many years to realise the fact. The question of light as a factor can be examined a little further. Within the two hours after dawn the feeding spell may hold for several weeks, as I said, but there are slight changes usually at intervals of two or three days, a shift of fifteen minutes or thirty minutes either way. These are real, not imaginary changes. For example one may, on one day, get two runs simultaneously at the start of the feeding spell, and the next day again two runs simultaneously – but fifteen minutes later. In detail I have been unable to relate light factors to these slight changes. Mornings may be dull, bright or misty, yet the detail of the feeding patterns seems unrelated. It may be that the pike begin to feed as a result of some more dramatic trigger mechanism, such as activity of the prey itself. But to argue thus is merely to beg the issue, were they responding to light? Martin Gay has recently argued (*Coarse Angler*, Dec. 1985) that the pike's biological clock is involved in some way. It seems much more likely to me that the local temperature, pressure and oxygen levels, all of which are directly related, are of importance. Given that a barometric pressure régime may well hold for several days, and that the temperature is related to cloud cover, winds, and other factors, the resulting oxygen level may oscillate through peaks and troughs which vary a little from morning to morning. During the winter all these factors are a little less variable, hour to hour, especially water temperatures and air temperatures. It seems to me that detailed variation within the broad feeding pattern is less in winter than in summer. And, of course, pike feed less in winter anyway, so that it is slightly more difficult to amass meaningful statistics such as how many runs make a feeding spell. It is very obvious that accurate observation of feeding patterns is best done when several rods are at work at the same time, as when friends fish together. This was why the original Cambridgeshire Specimen Group and the Cambridgeshire Pike Anglers were so successful.

Team fishing

Team fishing has provided us in Cambridge with quite definite proof of another interesting phenomenon. Whilst, for example, it is absolutely certain that on a particular fenland drain all the pike in one stretch will be on the feed from 8 a.m. to 9.30 a.m., it is equally true that a mile away on the same drain fish may be feeding strongly from, say, 11 a.m. to 1 p.m. One angler cannot be in two places at the same time, but two groups of anglers using the same techniques can fish from dawn until dusk in two quite distant localities. There is no question of error in these conclusions, the evidence from dozens of big pike taken being quite overwhelming.

There may be quite a simple explanation for this variation, namely, that the exact conditions which produce optimum oxygen levels for feeding may vary from place to place, being achieved at different times. Once again there is less likelihood of this in the uniformity that is winter.

Team fishing also enables one to consider another aspect of feeding patterns, namely, actual movements of the pike packs. All I have written in this chapter has been on the assumption that you are fishing in what I would call hotspots. But some anglers have suggested that the pike actually move about on routes, passing particular places (like the ends of gravel bars) at particular times. So, naturally, you'd have different feeding spells in different parts of the water. All my own experience, and my analyses of team efforts, convinces me that this only happens when pike are on a real hunting spree as a result of high barometric pressure; it is much more common for anglers on a water to get runs at more or less the same period of time – unless they are fishing where there are no pike.

CHAPTER TWO

Scavengers
supreme

The first printed book on angling (1486) by Dame Juliana Berners
contains an account of using herring deadbaits, and the hook rig used
was very similar to that 'invented' independently by Ray Webb and
published in our first edition (1971, figure 2B). This technique uses
a threaded trace and the hook in the head region of the herring. Berners
even describes a *buoyant* method of fishing the herring, using a float
between bait and lead: that piece of information should shake a few
modern would-be inventors!

Presumably, deadbaits on the bottom have been used ever since, but
they do not figure frequently in books, and in this century, at least,
the impression was very strongly held that pike took only living fish
or spinners and did *not* pick up dead objects from the bottom. The
Taylor brothers were really responsible for publicising the ledgered
herring method of angling, though others have tried to steal their
thunder. For a long time it was claimed that ledgered deadbaits really
only worked when some kind of pre-baiting had been done, something
we now know is quite false. Others claimed that, for example, the
Norfolk Broads could only be fished successfully with spoons and
livebait – at this very time Bill Giles and Reg Sandys were regularly
catching big Broads pike on herrings, and they were amongst the
pioneers in refining the method. There was also a period when a
concerted effort was made by some individuals to have deadbaiting
banned. This will amaze today's youngsters no doubt, but for those
of us around at the time it was a serious battle that had to be
fought – and won. The reason given for the ban was that too much
deep-hooking of pike went on. In truth, some anglers were jealous of
the results being achieved by others. However, it cannot be denied that
herring fishing was abused – some people who should have known

19

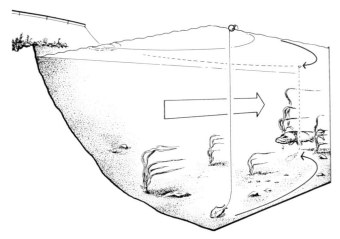

Drifting a float ledgered deadbait using current or wind drift.

better advised anglers simply to chuck out a herring and wait; if they wanted a big pike it would come eventually. It was never that easy, and it is silly to recommend to people that they use unthinking approaches. What I should like to do is take you, in the following paragraphs, through the developments and debates as they occurred, for much is still relevant to today's piking. And then I'll draw it all together, partly by way of contrast, with the position as it is today. Although we now seem to have it all sewn up and simplified, it is salutary to remember that everything changes and that what we consider firmly established today will be laughed at in twenty years' time. If this isn't strictly true some firm bastions will go at least. Let's begin with a quote from Ray Webb, describing how it all began for him and me.

'In the autumn of 1961 I was tackling up the heavy duty gear once again, though this time it was on the banks of an old clay pit in Yorkshire instead of the Witham and the bait, too, was different; a sizeable herring had replaced the small bar spoon of previous seasons and was now an up-and-coming lure for pike, after being publicised by Fred J. Taylor. It was also a new partner I had along with me, this occasion marking the first of a long and still continuing series of trips after pike with Barrie Rickards. He had suggested that I abandon the Witham watershed in favour of the Yorkshire fisheries. This was a move that was to prove its worth time and time again in the year ahead. With one rod out and fishing, my attention was focused on tackling up the second. On looking up I saw my float slide slowly along the surface for a couple of yards and then sink down out of sight. A solid resistance met the strike, and this in itself was quite an event for me in those days and something of a tussle ensued as an 11 lb pike was hauled protesting to the shore. This sort of weight ensured its classification as a day to remember and the situation was further improved shortly afterwards when I landed another big one of 9 lb. Two such pike in one day was enough to convince me that the ledgered deadbait technique was well worth studying and subsequent events have amply proved that this in fact is the case. It is no magical method answering all our piking problems since it fails completely, and often for no apparent reason, on many waters. Where it does succeed, the fish taken are of an extremely high average size. Pike of 3 or 4 lb will and do of course take a full-sized herring. I have seen on occasions times when a ledgered deadbait has produced a jack not much bigger than itself, but it is nevertheless true that as a rule the method yields a lot of double-figure fish with a good 20-pounder from time to time. On so many waters livebaiting turns up 4-pounders in numbers and wastes valuable baits intended for better things. A ledgered herring on a responsive water will usually cut these unwanted jack down in quantity. In addition, the availability of herrings for bait is another factor in their favour; very little time or effort is required to nip along to the local fishmonger to pick up a supply adequate enough for a day's piking.'

That day is also indelibly printed in my mind, and note how 9 lb and 11 lb pike were rated in those days. We were both experienced at spinning and livebaiting, and when we saw that float slide away we didn't even bat an eyelid – for about three seconds, that is. Then we roared, as if synchronised 'It's a *deadbait*, not a livebait . . .' and chaos ensued. That was the beginning of years of trial and error, analysis and reanalysis, and from it a series of truths and half truths slowly emerged.

Deadbaiting with a static bait can be desperately slow. Many anglers make no attempt to locate their quarry, but merely chuck out a herring and hope for the best. I had never met Fred Wagstaffe before the first National Association of Specimen Groups Conference at Chelsea in 1967, but we found we were in solid agreement on this issue. There are thousands of anglers throwing out thousands of herrings, half attended, for hundreds of thousands of fishing hours. The returns are relatively small, notwithstanding the numbers of 20-pounders reported in the angling press. (Have you noticed how many pike weigh exactly 20 lb? Mine usually weigh 19¾ lb!) The fundamental principle behind stationary herring fishing should be to find the pike, if at all possible before casting, and then concentrate on the tackle.

There is no doubt that ledgered herrings result in a good average size of pike caught, but I do recall an interesting observation that I made on the Great Ouse. On this water my smallest pike on herring is 5 lb, and I have had fewer fish for a higher average weight than with livebaits. But with livebaits, mostly ledgered, I have had just as many big pike, with the small ones thrown in to keep the slow spells interesting. I once had a 1 lb jack on one cast and in the same spot on the next cast had one of 23¼ lb.

On the other hand there is no need, in my experience, for stationary deadbaiting to be as slow as the Northampton pike specialist Fred Wagstaffe had found it to be on his waters. I remember being amazed during our fruitful discussions at Chelsea to find that his largest pike to this technique was, in 1965, around 6 lb and by 1967, 11 lb. Obviously he had been most unfortunate in his choice of waters, for there is no doubt at all that on some waters the fishing of static deadbaits is a waste of time.

Ray Webb and I had some very slow days, probably as a result of doing the job badly. One lovely winter's day in Norfolk we ledgered two herrings each, near some lock gates. The rods dipped towards the water like drinking fowl; the lines hung slackly; the wind was nil and the sun shone. Lunchtime came and went. We had fired the magic primus, but no Aladdin came. We settled back in our chairs surrounded by a vast array of dirty plates, pans, uneaten chips and onions, loaves, fat, and boxes of herrings. We fell asleep. About an hour later we were gently roused by faint gigglings and chuckles and looked round sleepily to find ourselves surrounded by a vast party of students, mostly female, who had come to see the lock gates and the machinery installed therein. The rods still dipped to the water, the lines were still slack, and so everything remained until dark, a fitting conclusion to fourteen hours of pure, immobile, unadulterated, winter sunbathing pleasure.

This is no way to fish for pike of course, even if it is the way that many people like. Fishing the same swim on an earlier occasion with the lock gates wide open and a full flood coming through I rolled two herrings loaded with Steuart multihook tackles around the bottom. It was really hard work involving a fair amount of casting, recasting, and tackle control in the turbulent current and entangling debris, but in very little time I extracted three double-figure fish, the best weighing 16½ lb. One of the best herring fishermen I know, Roy Hatherley of Edgware, fishes two rods, one ledgering which he recasts roughly every hour and one on float tackle arranged so that it drags very slowly through the swim either just on the bottom or just above it. He then works slowly downstream in a series of arcs with the float tackle, bringing the ledger rod along behind. The fish that do not like a moving bait often take the stationary one. The hook rig used is the standard Fred Taylor rig of two trebles along one flank of the bait. The moral is that unless you are absolutely certain that you are in the swim with a big pike it pays to move slowly and methodically, much in the way that Roy does. I remember once spotting a pike about 11 lb in the weirpool at Hempholme Lock on the R. Hull, and by a bit of careful work managing to wangle a herring so that it lay on the bottom about six inches in front of the fish's nose. It ignored the bait for about one and a half hours and then, presumably, the smell became too much for it, for it drifted off downstream to get out of the way. I think one and a half hours is about long enough to leave a bait out under most circumstances.

A pike of 26½ lb taken at long range on half bait under rough, south-westerly wind conditions.

Sprats

I am confining myself for the moment to talking about herrings, sprats and mackerel since most of my experience up to 1970 was with these easily obtained baits. On the question of large versus small deadbaits – in my case herrings versus sprats or chopped herrings – I think I would have plumped for the whole herrings until 1969, when events on some waters changed my mind about half-herrings and half-mackerels. On numerous occasions we have had a sprat on one rod and

I do not really think the returns have been as good as they might have been. Ray has already mentioned the clay pit at Newport in East Yorkshire, where we did a fair bit of deadbait fishing. Sprats here were a first-rate groundbait, but produced few pike except for a 6½ lb fish that we used to catch once a week. (We would put it in a keep net to stop it going back to eat all the groundbait.) This contradiction suggests that we did not fish the sprats properly, particularly as a number of pike caught on herring were stuffed full of sprats.

As can be imagined, we knew exactly where the pike were on this pond and, as on several other waters, experience has dictated our choice of hooking arrangements.

Multihook rigs

In general we found that fewer runs were actually obtained on multihook rigs than on a bait presented with just one treble hook stuck in it. The idea outlined by Ray, of having one or two trebles well towards the back of the deadbait and never nearer the head than the dorsal fin, clearly solves most problems. I was the chief sufferer from multihook rigs, including the Dave Steuart tackle, for I loved the theory and the whole idea of having plenty of hooks on the bait. I had fewer runs than Ray when fishing in the same swims, and in general finished up with smaller pike. On simple hook arrangements it is rare to get a run and have the pike drop the bait. Whilst the Steuart tackle is a really good rig for well-feeding pike, and I too can say that I have not once missed on the strike when using it, you do get a number of very short, very fast runs which drop the bait like a hot potato. These runs are so fast and so brief that it is quite impossible to get a strike in, even if float tackle is used.

I am also quite certain that a lot of pike pick up herrings loaded with multihook rigs and drop them quickly without producing more than the merest tremble on the float or twitch on the line. On numerous occasions I have found my herrings marked by the pike's teeth and yet no trace of a take has been seen. This rarely happens with herrings adorned with simple hook arrangements, and once the pike have made up their mind to take it they do just that, and do not let go until the angler unhooks them. The two popular ideas, that the angler cannot fish a herring badly, and that once the bait is lying on the bottom adorned with hooks nothing can go wrong, are quite incorrect.

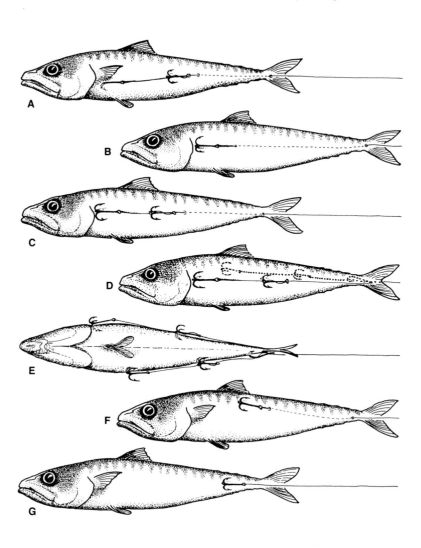

Deadbait hooking arrangements: A, B; early simple hook rigs used by the author on Newport Long Pond. C; 'standard' Fred J. Taylor arrangement. D, E; Steuart multihook rig using small trebles. F; one of the most successful simple hook systems, and one now used almost exclusively by the authors. G; emergency simple rig for the few waters where pike gulp down the dead-bait very quickly (see text). In these figures the dashed lines indicate where the trace is *threaded*, except in D where it merely indicates that portion of the trace at the back of the bait.

This is not to say that the pike is super-intelligent. They probably treat multihook rigs in exactly the same way as do eels, which I have actually seen in action. How often do eel anglers find that their quarry has taken a very neat bite or two out of the bait, exactly between the hooks? What eels do is this: they close their jaws on the bait and if they encounter the treble hook, instead of the flesh they expect, they simply shuffle along the bait opening and closing their jaws until both jaws feel and taste flesh. Then they take a bite. The point is simply that they see and smell dead fish, and they expect to eat dead fish, not loads of old iron. Pike-perch behave very similarly except when very small trebles are in use, when they will gulp in the lot.

Multihook rigs for pike should, of course, be constructed with very small trebles, at least as small as sizes six and eight. Nevertheless, the above remarks still apply – though if you want to catch good numbers of big pike, particularly from pike lairs and hotspots, then forget about multihook rigs. The pike do not like them, and I suspect that even though the pike's jaws are designed to be lacerated (by the very food they eat), they are probably still quite sensitive when feeding leisurely on static deadbaits. For many years I used multihook Steuart tackles on one rod and simpler tackles on the other, but have now completely abandoned use of the former.

My experience of far fewer runs on Steuart tackles is not confined to Newport in East Yorkshire, but applies quite spectacularly on the River Great Ouse where four times as many runs have been obtained on simple rigs than on Steuart tackles. The test, of course, is to use the correct Steuart tackle against a simple rig for months in the same swims; there is no doubt whatever about the conclusions to be drawn if the angler adopts this approach. Identical conclusions were reached on Hornsea Mere, where Ray did considerably better than his companions who were using various complicated rigs in the same swims (from the same boat in fact). In this case, and on other waters, it was found that float tackle and leads on the line were also detrimental to success. The shallower and smaller the water the truer this statement probably is, and the simpler the tackle the better the results.

I think the comparative Great Ouse results for part of the winter season of 1965 are useful to conclude this particular debate, but I would emphasise that the pattern obtaining there is quite typical of other waters and other seasons:

multihook rigs – twenty-six rod days – seven pike
simple rig (single treble) – fourteen rod days – twelve pike

I reckon the simple tackle to be between three and four times as effective as the multihook outfit, which more or less agrees with our results on most, but not all, other waters.

Swallowing on the spot

There is a very popular idea, connected with the foregoing arguments, that heavy pre-baiting with herrings and sprats cause pike to swallow the anglers' baits without bothering to swim off. In other words, that their normal caution has been allayed to a considerable degree and that they just sit on the bottom gulping down whatever is thrown in. This is utterly, completely and demonstrably wrong. The Hornsea Mere pike, and those in Newport Long Pond, were swallowing herrings without moving off long before many herrings had been thrown in. The 'problem' was there from the word go, and this has been our experience on a number of other waters, some of which had never seen herrings before. The answer is fairly simple, if not widely appreciated, and merely reflects the fact that the angler has been fishing in an individual pike's lair or in a pike hotspot. On most occasions pike *do* move off after mouthing the bait, but in the particular circumstances just mentioned a fair number of pike may feel no inclination or need to run at all.

Mackerel versus herrings

Mackerel have several distinct advantages over herrings. In the first place they are more solid, less easily broken up, and, in consequence, more easily cast. The hooks tend to take a good hold in the tough skin, and it becomes quite unnecessary to tie the bait on with nylon, crêpe paper, or rubber bands, unless one intends doing some real distance casting. What really interests me is that pike seem to prefer them to herrings, and there is no doubt at all that they have a distinctly more oily appeal than do herrings. The tail end of a mackerel really flies through the air.

The hook arrangements I have mostly used are shown in the illustrations and, clearly, there is no problem about when to strike when using a bait of this size. Assume that the pike is over 10 lb and strike as soon as it is running steadily off. It may be that you are uncertain how much weight your rod will cast. This problem is easily solved with half-baits: simply leave the hooks rather towards the tail and pare off strips until the best weight is found. Choosing the correct casting weight for your rod is much more difficult using whole herrings and mackerels! In fact, one often has to resort to throwing the bait out by hand, or using a casting stick.

Martin Gay with a firm, fit twenty-pounder from the Great Ouse Relief Channel.

Half-baits also release a more constant stream of oils and juices which may form a smooth area in the roughest of water conditions. The moment when a pike takes the bait in its mouth is often marked by a vast oil slick bubbling to the surface, giving the attentive angler some warning of events to come. All these factors, and particularly the pike's opinion, have caused several of us to make a marked swing over to mackerel fishing. The only snags are that mackerel are slightly less universally available than herrings, they are more expensive, and they go 'off' more quickly.

Suspended deadbaits

What of suspended deadbaits? How effective are they? I have formed a few ideas on suspended deadbaits, and am constantly irritated by people who say that choppy conditions are a prerequisite for success. But plenty of good pike have been caught on suspended deadbait when the water has been flat calm and the sun beating down, and from my own exerience I would draw no distinction between them at present.

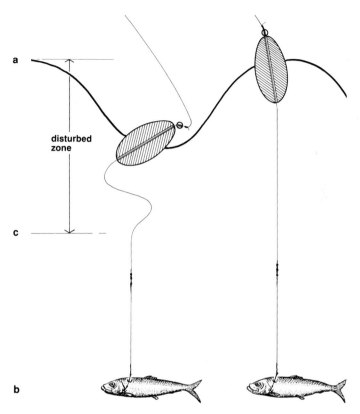

The action, or lack of it, of suspended deadbait fished in rough conditions.

On waters where choppy conditions result in better piking anyway, then presumably this applies to suspended deadbait as to any other method used.

However, choppy conditions do not result in a suspended deadbait flapping attractively up and down, except in very shallow water. The diagram explains what happens in deeper water: the distance ac represents the disturbed surface layer in which the float c and the line from a to c jerk up and down with the wave action. This happens so regularly and frequently with the wave action that the line between a and b (the suspended bait) remains more or less undisturbed, and the bait merely turns round very slowly. In these situations the pike knows very well that the bait is stone dead, and I should think the movement of the bait is so slow that it does not attract pike lying beyond its range of vision in the water concerned. (I presume they can feel vibrations from a greater distance than they can actually see.) No, pike take suspended dead fish because they see a dead fish lying in midwater and they can see no reason for not eating it. If you suspend a deadbait in really clear water, with the sun shining, you can actually see what happens to it even when the surface is quite rough. Only when very near the surface does the bait begin jerking about rather more quickly.

I have used all types of fish for suspended deadbaits, a half-ounce gudgeon resulting in a fish of 18¼ lb, and a 10 oz roach in a pike of 29 lb 10 oz. The first of these fish was taken only two feet deep in fourteen feet of water, and the second by swimming the stream about 4–6 in. off the bottom in ten feet of water. This raises the first point about actual techniques: the pike may be taking in quite a narrow depth band – possibly the depth at which their food fish are swimming – and this may be anywhere from the surface to the bottom in quite deep water. The float needed should be chosen so that it just supports the deadbait weight, or, in rough conditions, should be just

The author with a fish of 29 lb 10 oz, which fell to suspended 10 oz deadbait on a slow drift.

large enough to be seen in the waves. Probably I have used more dead roach and bream for this method of piking than any other, and wind drift (in still waters) can be used to work the bait and cover the water. By carefully positioning the treble hooks towards the head end of the bait an attractive (to us) sink and draw appearance can be achieved.

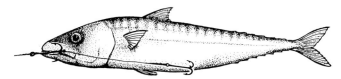

Bill Giles' deadbait hooking arrangement using large trebles, and thick Alasticum single strand wire: the tackle is retrieved slowly using sink-and-draw system (see text).

But considerable, if not equal success can be obtained by fishing a flat still water, with a floating line, and a deadbait suspended below a small float, however unlikely it may seem. Normally we set the deadbaits in a horizontal, so-called life-like position but events at various times have suggested that this is probably unnecessary. Good pike have fallen to baits hanging tail upwards or tail downwards! It takes a great deal of faith to fish suspended deadbaits in this manner, but it certainly assists casting. Very little distance can be achieved with a horizontally set bait.

The first time I saw suspended deadbait succeed in calm conditions was many years ago, when I fished a dead perch three feet deep in a twelve-foot deep swim in the 'Glucose' lake at Rawcliffe in the West Riding of Yorkshire. Nothing fell to my livebaits or plugs that day, but the suspended dead perch slid nicely away and yielded a 4¾ lb jack. A few years later I watched Bill Ellerker, the Hull angler, drifting herrings on a clay pit near Newport. His baits were set at seven feet

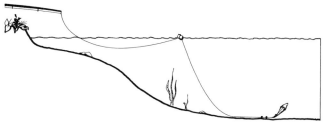

Float ledgered buoyant mackerel or herring.

in eight to nine feet of water, and whilst ledgered herrings, sprats and livebaits remained untouched all day long, the drifted herring contacted big pike twice, both unfortunately being dropped off just as they neared the net – a case of too early striking or too few hooks, whichever way you want to look at it. Today, that amount of information would have been enough to start me off investigating thoroughly, for I have learnt the hard way that there is no such thing as coincidence in angling.

A general rule with suspended deadbaits seems to be that the pike are either 'on' them, or 'off' them. Many anglers seem to think that livebaits in the same swims at the same time will always be better, but this certainly is not the case. Many a time it has been quite the other way round. Laurie Manns, Christine and myself were livebaiting on the Great Ouse with no success except for a couple of quick tugs. Laurie tried suspended deadbait on one rod and started taking fish regularly. We got the message then and finished up with eighteen good fish between us weighing over 100 lb. None fell to livebaits fished in the same swims and at the same depths. They remained untouched all day long.

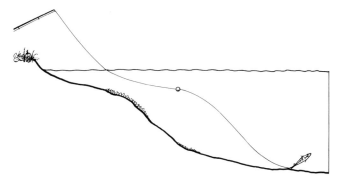

Using a sunken float set deep to avoid snaggy edges to a drop-off.

It could be added here that this kind of activity is not unique to pike: perch will occasionally take only dead lobworms, and I once shared a large catch of livebait with Rian Tingay, all of which fell to dead maggots, live maggots getting only very rare bites. I offer no real explanation as to why pike should prefer suspended deadbaits on enough occasions to make it a useful technique to know, but like so many other piking techniques, the important fact at the moment is that it *does* work well.

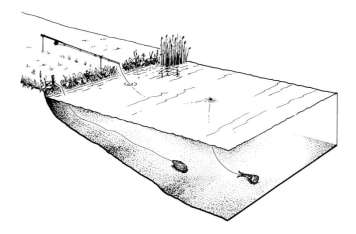

Using a 'rubby dubby' basket of chopped herrings to attract pike to a swim. Float ledgered deadbait is the tackle in use.

The trouble with piking is that there are so many unknowns; and half-baked, shallow theories concocted to explain various pike behaviour patterns (over-feeding and pike swallowing herrings, or rough water being necessary for suspended deadbait) I find rather irritating. Usually such theories are based upon a lack of facts and lack of experience.

Perhaps, purely in the realms of speculation, and in order to encourage the reader to keep an open mind, I can illustrate what I mean by 'unknown factors'. Have you ever spilt a gallon of maggots in the house? Well, Christine and I have done just that on three occasions, the last time being in 1967. We arrived back in the evening to find the house alive with maggots in almost every room. After the initial dismay we realised a quite amazing fact – on all three occasions the maggots were crawling round the house in an anticlockwise direction. Presumably, in the southern hemisphere, they would crawl the other way! This is the sort of behaviour I mean – totally unpredictable. How do we know, or how can we test, whether pike will pick up a ledgered herring with the trebles set in its left flank as opposed to its right? In still waters pike might possibly prefer to have the bank on their left, or in front of them, or behind them. The possibilities are endless, and, added to the variables that we *do* know something about, the possible combinations and difficulty of predicting behaviour are probably quite infinite. As I have already waded in up to my neck I think I will retire to the bank and get dried.

One of the greatest changes in piking in the 1980s has been the exploitation of more species of deadbaits than the traditional, though still effective, herring, sprat and mackerel fishing that I described above. In part, this has resulted from more varied species being available in the fishmongers, which in turn is a result of overfishing, commercially, of the sea (so that traditional English sea fish are less reliably abundant). Let's have a look at those various fish and their characteristics and effectiveness.

Flatfish

I first came across use of these almost twenty years ago, and before that I was aware that pike on the Yorkshire Derwent ate flounders, as indeed they do on the Great Ouse and some Fenland drains. Plaice, flounder and sole do catch pike, but their use has never really caught on. For a start they are difficult to cast, catching the wind quite badly, even in strips. At present we should look upon them as a change bait, or one to use when other baits have gone 'off' (though I shall have more to say on that aspect of piking towards the end of the chapter). A point worth remembering is that offcuts of many flatfish can be obtained for nothing from many fishmongers – heads, tail ends, wings and backbone. They are good for baiting up with or for making into fishcakes (more later!).

Sardines

Everything has a 'discoverer' and whilst Basil Chilvers 'discovered' half baits Bill Chillingworth did the same for sardines. Within a couple of trips of Bill using them I tried them myself. That was early in the 1970s and I have had many good fish on them since.

Sardines rank with mackerel as one of the very best of pike baits. I used to use them with a small snap tackle, the Ryder going through the tail, often tied on so that I could get several casts for close range fishing. (I once had four double-figure fish on one sardine, which must be something of a record: at the end, all I had was a string of vertebrae and a tail!) Now, thanks to a tip from Martin Gay, I put the Ryder through the eye and into the skull, which gives a much better purchase, especially for long range casting with heavy leads. I still use a small snap tackle.

Smelt

I get more runs on smelt than on any other bait. I also get more dropped runs than on any other bait, even when using quite sophisticated hook rigs. So what is potentially the very best bait of all actually ranks third in my book, behind mackerel and sardine. We used to get fresh smelt in Yorkshire from a lake leading off the Humber estuary, but we didn't use them for pike in those days. Later, in the early 1960s we were to do so in Fenland when we obtained them in tidal waters near King's Lynn and used them in the Relief Channel, but not as frequently as we should have liked to have done. Now you can often buy them by the stone in fishmongers.

I haven't mentioned their cucumber smell, which is considered by many to be their feature most attractive to pike (thereby belying those fools of scientists who think pike do not rely much on their sense of smell. How do they manage to scavenge so well?) Several years ago Neville Fickling, unable to get hold of some smelt, injected cucumber juice into a herring and caught a 20-pounder, among other fish. So it does look as though the aroma is one factor which draws the pike to smelt, and Neville was quite correct to draw attention to smelt as a top class bait.

Smelt, like trout, stay frozen and buoyant for much longer than other deadbaits. Should you be fishing 'free-line' you may need as many as four swan shot to hold down even a small smelt! They are also tough and may last any number of casts, although the stomach eventually comes apart.

Cod, haddock, gurnard and whiting

These are still change or bait-up baits, in the same class as flatfish. Some good fish have fallen to whiting, but my own experience is that they do not do as well as oily baits like herring or mackerel. When I used sprats a great deal we used to buy several pounds, and amongst them were tiny cod and whiting. I tried them but they never did as well as sprat, which is, of course, another oily fish.

Weaver and bass

Two light-coloured spiky fish these, and the weaver when alive has a nasty poisonous dorsal spine, as every sea angler knows. For some reason pike like weaver and I have caught some nice pike on them, including fish over 20 lb. When frozen and used as half baits they cast really well and have the tough skin of trout, smelt, eels – and bass. Small fresh bass are increasingly seen in fishmongers and, like flatfish, they tend to be very fresh. I have started to try them extensively but do not yet have much to report. They make excellent drift baits, staying as intact as red gurnard – these I have abandoned as really not very good (probably I shall regret that decision and may revoke it in the future!). As a small digression I should mention a couple of other rejects – squid and octopus. Whilst these do well at sea, and some pike anglers use them, I have yet to get a run. I *haven't* given them a proper trial.

Trout

This is another good bait, but grossly over-rated by some people for entirely theoretical reasons. In the face of the most contrary evidence – that many waters do not contain trout – the theory is that pike grow big and fat on trout and therefore must always prefer them. For a start, it is by no means certain that big pike in trout reservoirs grow that way solely because of a trout diet: those waters also have many good coarse fish, such as perch and eels, and big waters without trout also produce big fat pike (especially when they haven't been fished for a decade or two).

Trout are, nonetheless, good baits. They cast well, are tough, and I have had plenty of good pike on them with several over 20 lb. I recall once, on the Great Ouse as darkness fell, missing three runs on half a rainbow trout, tail end thereof. After the third run there was no flesh left, only two folds of skin, a backbone and tail – minutes later the indicator flew off for the fourth time and this time I connected with a fish that topped 20 lb. I had assumed it was a jack pike messing about with the bait.

Natural freshwater fish

There was a time when I used these almost exclusively, but I now genuinely feel they are not as good as certain sea fish deadbaits. That said, *all* freshwater fish make good deadbaits and many of them, like perch, are tough on the hooks, greatly assisting casting. They also make excellent suspended deadbaits, but I must emphasise that they need *not* be set horizontally. Anyone who has done much fish watching knows quite well that many fish drift about, head upwards or head downwards, quite commonly. Even as suspended deadbaits I do not rate them quite as highly as sprat or sardine, but they *are* better on the hooks. Wobbled or spun naturals I shall deal with in the chapter on lures, because it is a more mobile method of angling.

Eels

Savouring the moment, I have left these to the last because they are so good. Pike love eels, alive or dead. Most experienced anglers will have caught at least a few pike with eels, partly digested, hanging from their maws. They can be used as deadbaits in lengths of up to six inches or so, and they cast like a bullet. Getting them off the hooks is like removing Excalibur! Smoked eels also work well and pike certainly like the smokey flavour, as confirmed by their liking for kippers, which make both a good bait and a good additive. So at the risk of incensing today's eel lovers I suggest you freeze one or two of those bootlace jobs: I wonder if pike strips would make good eel baits?

I could go on and on about trying different species of fish as deadbaits. There is still a great deal of room for trials to be carried out. But it can become a fetish. One of the silly ideas I have frequently come across is 'mackerel are no use on this water'. Very, very often it is total nonsense. Only last winter (1985) I had a run on my first cast with half a mackerel on a water where the local pike anglers claimed that no pike had ever fallen to the bait. In truth they never used it, except at the beginning of their campaign when they used it wrongly. Let me put it quite bluntly – I have never, ever, found a water where mackerel fails. I have found a few waters where herring is better, especially when the herring is fresh and juicy, with a red head *and scales*. Did you know that the modern housewife does not realise that herrings have scales? This is because the commercial process which brings herrings to the fishmonger's slab is now a cruder, mechanical business which is harder on the carcass than in the past. The scales get lost!

In getting too fiddly about different species of bait we can easily lose sight of some real truths, that mackerel, sardine, smelt and herring are superb deadbaits anywhere, and that trout, eels and freshwater fish make excellent back-up baits or baits for special circumstances. We can also fail to investigate one or two other deadbaiting matters that do need looking at, such as . . .

Pre-baiting and groundbaiting

I used to try groundbaiting in such a way that it attracted (by smell) but didn't feed – as by wrapping the groundbait in wire netting and chucking it out on a rope. I was worried that it was possible to overfeed pike. I now think this is totally wrong in almost all circumstances. Pike cannot get enough food by scavenging. All that happens is that they grow big and fat on it! And they do get used to taking the bait quite happily. I have been loading reject bait and fish offal into one drain with great success and the fish have been putting on weight at not much less than 4 lb per annum, which I am sure is at least greater by half than the usual growth rate there. There's no problem at all with deep-hooked fish. One simply strikes at the very first sign of movement on the float.

Groundbaiting on the day, as with discs of frozen mackerel or herring, I am certain is very effective. I have caught numbers of pike with the discs inside their mouths, and the discs still cold having only just sunk. We ought to use discs as bait much more often than we do, or chunks of fish when we want a mighty cast. Incidentally, if a pike still has loose discs in its mouth upon capture it can hardly have been very worried during playing, otherwise it would have ejected them.

Groundbaiting can also be carried out by throwing in frozen balls. I had better explain that. Fish offal can be minced and mixed with ordinary groundbait to make fishcakes. Moulded into a fist-sized ball, with a stone in the middle, they can be wrapped in clingfoil to be frozen, and then used as groundbait. On being thrown out they sink (if you have the stone right!) and then slowly release smell and particles into the water over quite a long period. It takes at least an hour for such a ball to thaw completely. You can, of course, add all sorts of goodies to such a ball, such as pilchard (sardine) oil, cucumber juice or flavouring, and small pieces of chopped fish. Or blood.

Now there's something which hasn't been investigated properly. If sharks are really attracted to blood, why don't we try the same for pike? Ox blood and jellied ox blood can be bought, as can various powders, so I intend to try this more than I have done in the past. It seems unlikely to me that pike are *not* attracted by the smell of fresh blood.

The colouring of deadbaits is something that many of us have tried, and there is quite a bit of experimental work going on in this field at present. Personally, I do not yet accept the idea that colour changes are needed because a bait has been fished out. But I do feel that pike may like certain colours, and that this may differ from water to water.

One certainly hears of red baits being favoured on one water, and blue on another and so on. I haven't tried coloured baits for a long time now, deeming it unnecessary, but I am prepared to keep an open mind on this one . . .

Whilst thinking experimentally, let me suggest something else that needs looking at – the entirely artificial bait, the super-boilie. I have a feeling that something from the HNV stable, almost tennis ball size, in a variety of colours and flavours, would work well for pike. Hooking would be no problem, nor would casting (a tennis racket?). And groundbaiting would be child's play, if expensive child's play. Pike pick up boilies quite happily as they used to pick up balls of white paste equally happily. Perhaps we should give them their own boilies.

The last word on hook rigs

Use of deadbaits can be said to be in a healthy state in that not only is there a good sound basis of excellent baits, but there is still great scope for experiment. Hooking rigs have, however, reached a stage where I feel development has stopped or, to put it more bluntly, should stop, because in the snap tackle we have what amounts to a very, very good rig, in my opinion the best that there is, or has been.

I do not mean that remark about stopping experimentation very seriously. One should always experiment. But the word experiment implies trying something out with good reason, and that the research is controlled – as in the case of Vic Bellars' rigs which I shall discuss later on. What it *doesn't* mean is doing something because it is the 'in' thing, or because it sounds good in theory. The diagram illustrates the snap tackle that I regard as the 'ideal' rig. I use it for 99% of my piking and its use has resulted in thousands of pike – almost a thousand over 10 lb in fact. To put it negatively, it can't be bad. To put it positively, it is damned good. And it really annoys me when I hear the rig denigrated by pike anglers who, if they have anything in common, share a lack of experience. As I pen this it is August 1985, and during the summer, for want of a better word, I have actually missed only two runs: one pinched the sardine; the other snapped on the strike due to one of those incredible overnight loss of line strength incidents. And in that time quite a lot of fish have come to the net.

Hook sizes should be 6 – 10, depending upon the bait and the quarry. Larger hooks are entirely unnecessary except on lures and on wobbled deadbaits. Some superb hooks are made today, such as by Ryobi-Masterline and by Partridge, and these are the ones that I use. They are very strong, some almost excessively so, and they have small, neat barbs. I am totally opposed to the use of barbless hooks for this kind of fishing although I use micro-barbs for trouting (of my own construction) and the same for tiddler snatching (i.e. roach fishing). I am quite unconvinced by stories of anglers losing no more fish than on barbed hooks. They simply haven't thought it through: *how do they know?* Barbless hooks make unhooking pike easier and by the same token the fish can unhook itself more easily during playing. There's really no argument about this – the fact that someone is skilful enough to avoid this happening most of the time is quite irrelevant. This is also the reason why so-called semi-barbless trebles are used: a barb is needed for the hook that goes into the deadbait – otherwise it would fall off!

Nor is it necessary for the Ryder hook to be *fixed*. This is another old wives' tale that seems entrenched because, years ago, a couple of famous but not so experienced pike anglers said that the hook would slide under pressure and fail to hook. Rubbish! There is, in fact, a good reason for having a sliding Ryder, quite apart from the ability to adjust quickly and accurately to different bait sizes. Consider the 'fixed' hook. If *one* of those six points hits bone on the strike, *none* of the other five will move a millimetre, and *all* will fail to get a hook hold. With a sliding Ryder hook there is a greatly increased chance of the rig relocating itself and taking a good purchase. This, in fact, is what often happens in practice; both trebles may end up close together, or be nine inches apart with independent grip. Practice is what makes successful piking, not armchair theorising. Go fishing, catch, then analyse what is good and what works.

There are now some good trace wires on the market. I use Tidemaster, Marlinstrand and Alasticum, but there are others equally as good. I'd be happier if they were less springy and could be twisted up more easily where attached to the swivel or lower treble. I'd also like to have a nice simple-to-use glue to dab on the twisted portion to give it a good finish. If such a glue were available – and it isn't – then the twisted portion need be no longer than ¼ in. I do expect that in the next decade we'll get new types of wire: thinness isn't a problem anymore, but suppleness and flexibility and softness are.

The length of the trace wire needs to be about twelve inches, give or take an inch or two. Yard-long traces are quite unnecessary and, once again, use of such traces is simply fetish-following or theory gone mad.

Richard Walker said yard-long traces were necessary on Loch Lomond, so everyone starts using them! The 'theory' behind the use of long traces is that they are needed to avoid break-offs in amongst boulders. In fact, no strength or length of trace will help unless it is at least half an inch thick. The trick when fishing such swims is to know the depth exactly and to fish with the deadbait lying just on the bottom, leaded down sufficiently in conditions of high wind or current drift. Long traces on the bottom do not assist in avoiding snags, nor do they help you get out should you become hooked around a boulder. Indeed, a long trace lying on the bottom actually *increases* your chances of becoming snagged up in the first place. Finally, use of a long trace in deadbaiting makes it less simple to switch to livebaiting or spinning, and for flexibility in piking that in itself is important. The short trace can be used for livebaiting as well as deadbaiting, which the long trace cannot.

I have not, in any of the foregoing, written much about the tackle – ledger or float – that can be used with deadbaiting. This I do in later chapters, notably that dealing with tackle and techniques, but also that describing livebaiting. Here I want to document one of the changes that has taken place since the 1960s. At that time the bulk of piking in the nation was done with floats. Not only that, but mostly it meant shallow-fished livebaits below a *Fishing Gazette* slit bung. In the first edition I argued strongly for ledgering as one of the improved techniques, both for livebaiting and deadbaiting; and today, should you do the round of pike fisheries, you will find that a sizeable majority use ledgering techniques. In fact, the matter has gone to the other extreme and has rather unhealthy aspects to it, such as slavishly ledgering in rock-strewn swims. I do not flatter myself that it is I who have influenced the change. Rather, this sort of piking is an offshoot of modern carp fishing; when the summer is over the anglers simply add a wire trace, a fish bait, keep the Optonics, and continue fishing as before. It is unlikely that such a mental approach will lead to new discoveries in deadbaiting. Despite this reservation deadbaiting today is in a healthy state with simple, efficient equipment catching a great many pike.

As a final remark, a postscript as it were to this scene, I want briefly to discuss two further developments with respect to deadbaiting. One is the use of Vic Bellars' rigs, the other the use of hair rigs. Let me say immediately that I cannot see the point of hair rigs. I find them totally unnecessary in my own fishing – and some friends did try them the very moment they became established on the carp scene. They catch fish, but then so do the methods and approach I have described above. Bellars' hooks are good. I have discussed them with Vic several times and I think it is true to say that he considers them no more efficient, but no less, than a small hook snap tackle. In effect, the Bellars' hook has two upstanding hooks, whereas the snap tackle has four. But Vic prefers single hooks to trebles. I don't think that he would claim his rigs are any more 'instant' on the strike, unlike the claims of some people who have used them. With small baits of 5 oz or less (more usually less) nothing is *more* instant than a snap tackle. As far as sheer hooking ability is concerned I still sense that the snap tackle is the better rig. One of the original points about the Bellars' hook was that the deadbait needed to be only lightly nicked so that, on striking, the hooks would pull clear of the bait. This is an entirely unnecessary requirement in my opinion. I often tie my deadbaits on so that I get them back, and so that the pike cannot fiddle them off the hooks, which they do attempt to do on occasions. I have had thousands of pike on baits which have been firmly fixed to the hooks and I can vouch for the fact that with normal baits it makes no difference at all. Of course, if you wish to encumber yourself with complicated 'theories' . . .

Deadbait fishing for pike is for me the most enjoyable technique of all. I have done a great deal of livebaiting, which is by far the most productive method, and a vastly greater amount of lure fishing, but the great moment for me is when a totally static, lifeless rig, starts to move. There can be no mistaking the take. You're in business, and it's entirely up to you then whether you do it wrongly or correctly. The fighting ability of pike has a say, of course, but I'll discuss that factor in Chapter Eight.

CHAPTER THREE

The pike's natural food

The simple reason why livebaiting is the most successful piking technique is that the pike spends almost all its feeding time looking for live fish and thus is more easily conned by a bait that is alive. Encumbrances on the prey, such as hooks and trace, really go unnoticed by the pike because it does a great deal of its fish-catching in thick weed beds and is quite used to taking in a mouthful of weed. For the same reason the resistance and pull of the angler does not strike it as all that unusual. The livebaiter's approach is thus a very natural one.

Many anglers have had a small fish snatched from their roach fishing tackle. In fact, one of my earliest piking colleagues, Mac O'Donnell, used to fish for roach, hook one, and then simply leave it in the swim until it was taken by a pike! We weren't into wire traces in those days, and quite a few were lost as they bit through the line. But it did lead Ray Webb and I, at a much later stage, to try free-lining for pike, especially as that technique was in vogue in all other angling at the time – what a contrast to today, where you are frowned upon if you use leads under 4 oz.

On 12 June 1970, my birthday, I was using a very large, black rubber eel for pollack off the rocks bordering Clew Bay in Ireland. But all the time I was swinging this artificial bait around – on my pike tackle, incidentally – I was thinking what a really superb bait it would make for pike. Needless to say, with this attitude of mind, I caught no pollack. I shall return later on to the relationship of large pike and eels, a subject well worth exploring further: suffice it to say at the moment that the thought of using a small eel on free-line tackle dismays me. However, as far as all other livebaits are concerned, free-line fishing provides one of the simplest and most deadly piking methods.

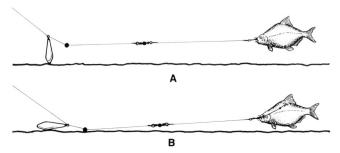

Lip-hooked and snap ledgered livebait tackle.
A is the author's preferred method.

It is probably fair to say that very few anglers use free-line or ledgered livebait techniques, despite the fact that both methods are almost always vastly superior to normal float-fished baits. I can recall only two articles in the angling press during the last ten years or so which dealt with ledgered livebait as a technique and none dealing with free-line fishing before 1970, when Jim Gibbinson of Essex began refining our techniques on some large reservoirs. Perhaps it will be of some interest to hear how we came to use the methods in our own fishing. I should preface my remarks by saying that we did not discover these methods – I believe that both are described somewhere by Bickerdyke himself.

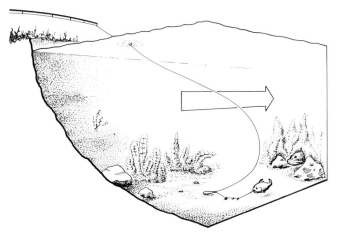

Holding a ledgered livebait in position in a snag-ridden swim and moderate current conditions.

As always, Ray Webb and I arrived at our findings by the wrong method. What we should have said was that since rod, line and hook are basic to all other methods of fishing (fly fishing, spinning, specimen hunting generally) why not pike fishing? In fact, I *began* by using small ledgered livebaits on Carlton Towers in West Yorkshire quite a number of years ago. This was summer piking, and the problem was to get the bait well out into a small hole in the weeds and to hold it there. The first surprising fact was that the livebait, provided it was under 4 oz or so, did not pull line off the reel but sat quite still on the bottom. I later confirmed this on the Market Weighton Canal in the East Riding where I was able to watch the bait 'in action'. The second most important factor was that the number of pike taken increased fourfold. I attributed this, at the time, to the fact that I had placed my bait exactly where I wanted it and where it remained relatively weed-free. Encouraged, however, I began using ledgered livebait all over the East and West Ridings of Yorkshire in waters varying from deep clay pits to shallow weedy waters. I now know that most of the waters I fished did not contain big pike. Nevertheless the *numbers* of fish taken were far in excess of the numbers caught by other anglers fishing the waters at the same time. Let me hasten to add at this point that where big pike *are* present the method is still very effective when compared to the more usual approaches. Nothing fancy is required in the actual makeup of

The author's first twenty-pounder, 23¼ lb to be precise. The technique used was ledgered livebait.

the tackle. An Arlesey bomb or swan shot ledger slides on the line and is stopped with a shot fairly close to the normal wire trace. The bait should be lip-hooked: if hooked near the dorsal fin it merely lies on its side on the bottom. If a treble hook is used several small livebaits can be used at the same time, giving the effect of a small shoal of fish.

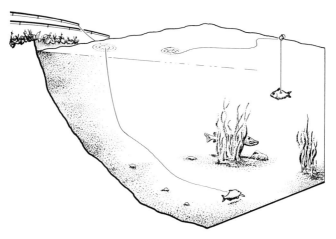

Free-line livebait tackle (nearest) and 'standard' shallow fished, suspended livebait using floating line and small sliding float.

When I first demonstrated ledgered livebait to Ray on the Great Ouse we were having a rather slow day, and by 4 p.m. we hadn't had a single run on herrings. We then sent my wife, Christine, to a near-by drain to catch some livebait. She quickly bashed out half-a-dozen smallish roach and suggested that we try ledgered livebait. The first cast produced a 12 lb fish to my rod. Ray, duly converted, evolved the free-line technique in a matter of days by the simple process of getting rid of the lead altogether. One of the difficulties with ledgered livebait, you see, is that the lead weight very often finds the snags, particularly when a fish takes.

On one of the early sessions at Carlton Towers my chosen swim was a mere 18–24 in. deep, liberally dotted with soft weeds, and surrounded by dense *Potamogeton* and *Elodea* beds. Several traditional livebait bungers had been through the swim during the day, including myself, and a fair bit of spinning had been carried out. Ten minutes after casting out a small roach, lip-hooked, and with a half ounce Arlesey bomb on the line, I got a real sizzler of a run. The pike took about ten yards of line before I caught up with it mentally, banged in the pickup of the Triplex reel and struck violently. There was a boil and an explosion of spray deep in one of the weed beds, and the Arlesey bomb shot up into the air at least eight or nine yards away from the fish! Everything, but everything, got tangled up in weed, but after a lot of heaving and tugging, my first pike to ledgered livebait, on my first cast to that method, finished up on the bank. I had another four fish out of the one swim that afternoon, all to the same technique, largest 4 lb. No other pike were taken on the water all day.

It seemed to me at the time, and on subsequent equally successful trips, that the pike in such shallow water were frightened of huge bungs and huge splashy spinners. Later experience with other piking techniques, such as ledgered herrings, bears this out. It *pays* to be as simple as possible with tackle arrangements, and as quiet as possible on the banks. Occasionally, even fairly commonly, such care doesn't matter, but mostly it does and I'm careful all the time as a matter of course.

Free-line tackle hardly demands illustration since the reel line terminates in a trace and hook, either treble or large single as preferred. Obviously, free-lining is carried out at short range up to, say, 25 yards. If more distance is required, or if the current is too strong, it becomes necessary to revert to ledgered livebaits. Addition of a swan shot ledger can be carried out without unshipping the gear although, indeed, this is easy enough! If a few float rubbers have been threaded on the line

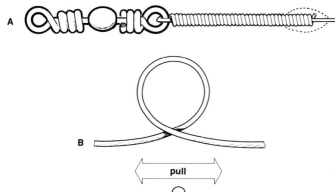

A, cabled wire attached to swivel; dashed lines indicate position of a small blob of Araldite. B, C, the way in which dangerous kinks develop in some cabled and single strand wires.

initially a float can be added if required. There is no doubt in my mind that free-lining produces more and better runs than does ledgered livebait: both are superior to float-fished baits when the pike have been accurately located but are not necessarily feeding strongly.

All livebaiting methods produce their share of 'killed' baits. This occurs when a fish swims up to the bait, clamps on it hard and then immediately drops it for no obvious reason. I have watched this behaviour on Wicken Fen in Cambridgeshire and it really is an astonishing sight. Sometimes a pike will kill a bait, swim away for a few yards, and then turn round and take the (now) deadbait without further hesitation. This is as true when ledgering as it is of float-fished livebaits. For some reason possibly connected with resistance, 'killed' baits are less common when free-lining than with any other method. I shall return to the contrast in behaviour between pike which are in their lair (for want of a better word) and pike which are actively hunting, whether singly or in packs. I mention it here since in my experience the greatest number of 'killed' baits (that is, without a run developing) occur when the angler is fishing in a pike's lair. The fact that pike *have* a specific lair can be easily established by the frequency with which a fish, returned to the water, is caught again in the original swim, even though this may be hundreds of yards away – in the case of one Hornsea Mere pike almost a mile away. It seems reasonable to me that a pike in its lair, not really hungry, would object to a precocious little roach swimming about and might be expected to deal it a fair old chomp – and then leave it until it was hungry. Or until the eels found it, which then raises other possibilities concerning pike, eels and night fishing!

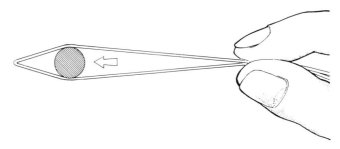

A way of taking out a less serious kink in trace wire than that depicted in the diagram (C) on page 55, using a round cross-sectioned object such as a ball-point pen. Not to scale.

One or two points might be emphasised on the subject of ledgering and free-lining with relatively small fish. Firstly, when free-lining in either shallow water or deep, still water or running, the bait always behaves in the same way – it swims to the bottom. This immediately overcomes one of the piker's main problems, namely, that of getting the bait down to where the pike are *most* of the time. Secondly, any of the usual bite indicators can be used – silver paper, electric bite alarm, empty spool etc. As free-lining is done at short range it is rare to get a take which does not give a visible indication. I have not fully explored the use of large livebaits on free-line tackle but my experience at the moment is that bream of half a pound or so either continue to pull off line quite strongly or else rapidly go to weed. Bream are of course first-rate livebaits, every bit as good as dace in my view, though I cannot comment on that reputedly good bait, chub. If I had to pick one type of livebait only I'd plump for a bream of around 6 oz. For a start they look bulky for their weight. More important, on the Great Ouse and some Irish loughs, the pike follow the bream shoals. Pike, unlike many anglers, love little bream.

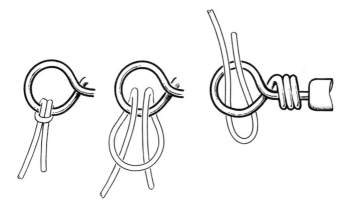

Alternative cabled Alasticum knot to that depicted in the diagram on page 47. Shown completed prior to twisting for approximately half an inch.

Earlier in this chapter I noted that if a ledgered livebait is fished on an ordinary snap tackle, or is hooked near the dorsal fin instead of in the upper or lower lip, then it merely lays on its side on the bed of the lake: a most unlikely way of getting results, and one we condemned as useless.

That was the position until the 1969 winter season when Hugh Reynolds began fishing the ledgered livebaits attached as normally to a simple snap tackle. As predicted in an earlier paragraph the baits lay quite still on the bottom, on their sides in fact. But this did not stop him getting some perfectly sizzling bites and some very good pike, the best, if I remember rightly, going well over 20 lb. Those fish were taken in eight feet of water at fairly close range, say less than twenty-five yards, on a still water near Cambridge. More important, however, they were caught at a time when the usual ledgered herrings and float-fished livebaits, fished in the same swims, produced little in the way of success. Hugh's pike had an average weight, in the first three months of that season, of 19 lb, a feat I have never before or since seen equalled. And the average was based on more than a handful of fish!

A further point, which we hardly dare mention these days, was that the water in question had rarely produced fish to ledgered livebaits previously, and had joined the short list of still waters where the technique seemed to be a failure. Unfortunately we have not had the opportunity to extend Hugh's experiments. As the reader will be aware by now, I do not spend a great deal of time 'bung' fishing for pike; that is, using a large float fixed a short distance of two to three feet above a (usually) small livebait! However, if it becomes necessary I will use such techniques with the best of them and before going on to discuss more sophisticated methods of float-fishing livebait it might be a help to describe some circumstances where the traditional method actually works quite well. This is in solidly weeded waters.

By this I mean shallow waters where the surface is weed from bank to bank, whether it be *Potamogeton* leaves at intervals of a few inches or thicker, softer, weedgrowths. Pike live quite happily in waters like this, and, as usual, manage to reach double figures or even 20 lb occasionally. I think we can learn a fair bit by watching and catching pike in weeded waters, and it is a fact that in many waters pike often hunt right in the thick of the weeds and not merely round the fringes of weed beds. This is where the angler fishes, so there is sometimes a world of difference between what the pike like and what anglers like.

Up in Yorkshire we used to fish the *Potamogeton* beds at Eastrington pits near Howden with thick line, a large bung set only three feet deep, and a snap tackle and livebait. The procedure was quite simple; we heaved the tackle into the weeds and we caught plenty of pike which were landed trailing ten feet lengths of weed stalks in their mouths. But a pike only needs to see you once, or be frightened by a heavy footfall or dropped oar, and you can usually say goodbye for a while. I have always advocated a far more cautious approach to piking than is practised by most anglers. And remember too that a pike does not always charge away when it has been scared. If you watch closely a fish that has definitely seen you, the very edges of the dorsal fin can be seen to make minutely agitated movements. The fish is keyed up to go, and at the next violent movement which you make, it does just that.

There are other occasions when I would use a shallow-fished live (or dead) bait, but not under a large bung. Those are the times when big pike are feeding very close to the surface over deep water. The line is set to float by rubbing it with 'Mucilin' or E.T. floatant, and the smallest float needed to support the bait is set *sliding* on the line even if I intend fishing less than two feet deep. But how does one fish sliding pike floats? It is my intention at this point to describe what I think is one of the most versatile livebait tackle rigs in existence, an outfit that whilst being thoroughly efficient in its prime purpose, can also be very quickly adapted or changed to suit most livebaiting problems.

Stop knots

Assuming that the rod has been put together and the line threaded through the rings, the next requirement is a stop knot on the line set roughly at the depth to be fished; it can be adjusted when the whole rig is assembled. Stop knots made of rubber bands soon perish, or work loose, and the best material is either nylon monofil about 6 lb b.s., or thick cotton. I have used nylon monofil for years and the only drawback I can think of is that if pulled too tight it tends to weaken the reel line,

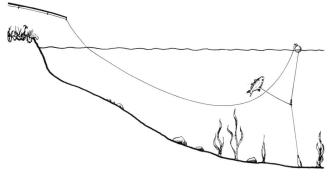

Paternostered livebait shown in act of tangling a badly sunken line. Such tangles result in bite-offs in the event of a pike taking the bait.

by decreasing its diameter locally. The knot itself is crude but effective; simply tie one granny knot after another until the bunch of knots is rather less than the size of the pin head. Practice determines how tight to set it – about three minutes' practice in fact! The loose ends are then cut back to about 1 in. lengths which tend to stand proud of the reel line. A stop knot of this kind flies easily through the rod rings, unlike one made of rubber band, and if well tied in the first place can be left on the reel line for weeks or months.

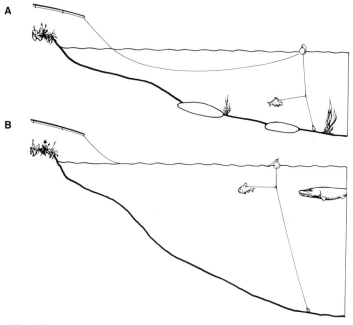

A, using paternoster tackle to anchor the bait in snag-ridden water. B, paternostering close to the surface in deep water.

If you are a particularly fastidious person with strong objections to scruffy knots, then the standard Billy Lane sliding float stop knot can be used instead. To make one of these, requiring a little more practice perhaps, a loop of 6 lb b.s. line is laid alongside the reel line, and then one end is coiled around the loop five or six times before passing the same end through the remaining part of the loop. The other loose end of line is then pulled tight, and the fingers used to control carefully the shape and tenseness of the knot. The end product is a relatively long knot of coils, with two loose ends which can be trimmed down as before.

Cotton knots may rot before several months have passed but this hardly seems a serious criticism of them! The cotton is rather easier on the reel line than is nylon monofil, but does not stand proud of the reel line when trimmed. However, the same bunched-up knot can be constructed and in the arrangement described below it is not necessary anyway to have stiff ends of the line built into the knot. I shall preface further remarks by saying that the kind of detail I am describing here, reflecting an attention to detail in my own fishing, is critical to successful pike angling. There is nothing sillier than having the depth fixer go wrong just when the pike are coming on the feed in a narrow depth band.

Stop knot bead

Having fixed the stop knot the next job is to slide a small bead, say less than a quarter of an inch in diameter, on to the line. There are beads and beads and beads, and you can safely assume at the moment that the ones sold in fishing tackle shops are unsuitable. Almost all of them have too large a hole through them, and in any event the tackle shop beads are probably sold for constructing spinners. I get my beads from Woolworths by buying a 'pearl' necklace of several strings' width. The cost is quite modest, and the necklace yields hundreds of beads from quite small, say ⅛ in. in diameter, up to a ¼ in. The hole is exactly right for nylon monofil from 10 – 15 lb b.s. Slightly larger holes can easily be made if required by working them with the point of a treble hook. Briefly test that the bead is stopped by the knot, though it becomes second nature after a while to get it right first time, and you are ready for the float.

Floats

Mostly the floats we use are 1 in. and 2 in. diameter; round floats with a hole straight through the middle. No slits or wires are needed: the stop knot arrests the bead and the bead stops the float. However, the beauty of this system is that any old floats you may have, or may find on the bank, can easily be converted, or even used directly, for the simple reason that the diameter of the bead is usually much greater than the diameter of any wire rings or loop attached to pike floats. *Fishing Gazette* floats can be turned upside-down when light conditions demand a dark float. Fire orange and yellow are two all-round colours for the float top, but white ones are useful sometimes. Providing one sticks to the basic idea of choosing the smallest float for the job, this business of float shape and colours is definitely of secondary importance. For one thing, light conditions change so quickly in winter that it becomes a bit of a fiddle changing floats.

Below the float, at varying distances from the wire trace, I pinch a swan shot which prevents the float from sliding down, during casting, over the swivel to the bait and hooks.

Snap tackles

Lastly there is the trace and hook system itself. There is, of course, an almost infinite variety of possible hook arrangements, and many possible trace materials, but the tackle I now use a great deal is the oft-maligned snap tackle designed so many years ago by Alfred Jardine. It is surprising, in view of the awful hammering the snap tackle has received from angling writers, that many experienced pike anglers came back to using them after trying and rejecting many other outfits. Dennis Pye, I believe, has always used them and I remember Bill Chillingworth and myself reverting to using them several years ago, after years of single treble rigs and multihook rigs.

Snap tackle hooks should be small, sizes six and eight, the trace wire fine, preferably dark-coloured, and supple. Shop-bought snaps rarely measure up to these requirements, probably most brands being much too thick in the wire of both trace and hooks. It *is* possible to buy snap tackles on fine wire, Stiletto being one make, but they take some finding in all except large tackle shops. Yet other snaps have much too short a trace wire; a 30-pounder could gulp down the whole rig, and this is something I am just not prepared to risk. So many other things can go wrong during piking that we may as well iron out the problems over which we do have some control. So I now make my own snap tackles of cabled wire, size six and eight trebles, and size six and size eight Ryder hoods. A swivel at the other end completes the tackle. Cabled wire is superior in several respects, for it is thinner and more supple, retains its dark colour indefinitely, and kinks much less easily. Hooks (except the Ryder hook) and swivels can be attached either by using brass crimp-on sleeves, available in most tackle shops, or by twisting the wire. The last method is perfectly adequate. Amongst my own angling companions anyway Basil Chilvers tried it first, and swiftly converted us from crimp-on sleeves even though these had never failed us. Richard Reynolds adds a spot of Araldite resin to the end of the twisted portion, thus lessening the risk of the connection untwisting. However, it never does untwist! The Ryder hook is slid into position *before* the swivel is attached. Suitable trace lengths are about 12 in. Traces should be ruthlessly abandoned to the tackle box if they become kinked in the manner depicted in the diagram. The effect of such kinks is to reduce the breaking strain of the wire by about 80 per cent, and whilst single-strand Alasticum is even more prone to such kinks, it *does* happen fairly often to the cabled variety.

Some types of trace wire sold are much too thick or shiny, or both. There is one kind of plastic-coated wire, which looks most attractive in the shops but which is useless for anglers who go pike fishing more than two or three times a year. At the slightest provocation from pike's teeth the plastic shreds off the wire, resulting in a close resemblance to 'Hairy Dan' string.

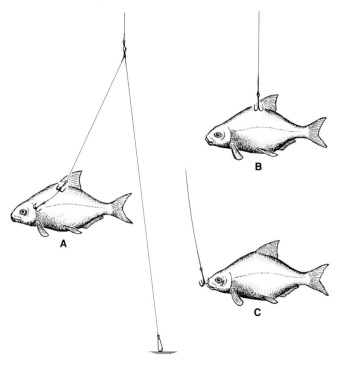

Paternoster rig detail using swivel with snap tackle (A), single treble hook near dorsal fin (B) and lip-hooked livebait (C). Not to scale.

To sum up then, we have now 'built' a very good tackle arrangement with a sliding float, stop and bead, swan shot, and at the bottom a snap tackle with small hooks and fine wire. What can we achieve with this rig? Firstly, it is possible to fish simple free-roving livebait at *any* depth. The stop is more easily slid along the reel line when the latter is wet, so a short false cast (without the bait) is made on to the water and the tackle retrieved. Or one can lick the line! The exact depth required can then be set, and here I use the five-foot rod joints as a reasonable guide. The Dennis Pye system of fishing the reedy margins of shallow Broads-like waters can be carried out by setting the float from twelve inches to two feet deep. A dumb-bell float can be used if preferred, although I have never really been able to understand the theory behind the use of dumb-bell floats.

Should the angler wish to change from fishing a two-foot deep marginal swim to searching a twenty-foot deep hole, the stop knot can be adjusted accordingly. It takes but a few seconds.

Paternoster rigs

I have now led us, logically, from free-lined and float fished livebaits, through 'bung' fishing to more sophisticated methods of sliding floats and paternostered rigs. I still use most methods as occasion demands, but have increasingly depended in recent years on the float paternostered technique. This I feel we have to a fine art and, except on the shallow waters I discussed earlier, I think it is the method I usually now opt for, certainly as a starter. The diagram illustrates the basic points. The float itself is, naturally, as small as you think you can get away with; and the lead is as light as necessary. Those considerations do not stop me using paternoster leads over 2oz, or large floats in deep and windswept waters.

Certain tricks of the trade are important. For example, the distance between swivel and stop shot or ledger stop should be 50 per cent or more greater than the length of the wire trace. This prevents the bait swimming upwards and hanging on the stop. (If a take occurs when this happens the pike bites through the reel line!) In warm weather certain species, such as rudd, should be lip-hooked because they have an almost uncontrollable tendency to swim upwards if back-hooked, commonly entangling the rig. An alternative method, a rather clumsy one but one which works, is to tie the paternoster line to the hooks. Two disadvantages attend this system; the bait has a tendency to fall off, and the pike needs more time to mouth the bait. Such tackle does cast well, however, because the bait doesn't slap about during the cast. I used to think that the weight of the lead was important in the sense that it should be as light as possible. Now, I'll quite happily use heavy leads.

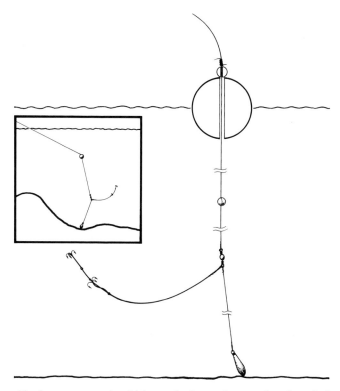

A good basic paternoster rig which can also be used as a sunken float rig (inset), providing a heavy enough lead or small enough float is chosen.

In the 1980s sunken paternoster rigs became very popular, and have been re-invented several times. For me they were discovered by Dave Steuart in the 1950s. Two great advantages accompany use of sunken floats. One is that it is not necessary to measure the water depth so precisely. The other is that surface drift is avoided somewhat, so that you can, if you wish, anchor the bait in one place. At the same time the line between float and rod should not be allowed to sink too deeply otherwise snags will be located with unerring accuracy. In fact it is a great help if the line goes tightly from the float to the reel and the indicator/clip system in use there, even if it means pulling the float towards you a little (not that you can see it, of course).

Various complicated versions of the float paternoster rig have been devised in recent years, and widely published, as in the *Pike Anglers' Club* magazine. Broadly, I have no use for them. I hasten to add that I do not intend to denigrate their designers in any way, but for my piking the methods I have described here have not only sufficed but have succeeded well. I am, I hope, always prepared to introduce change with good reason, but sometimes I do feel that the problem designed to be overcome is, in reality, an imaginary problem. But let me not discourage you . . .

Trolled livebaits

Almost twenty years ago Ray had a holiday in Holland, chasing carp if I remember correctly. He came back with stories of a crazy method of piking whereby the angler rowed a boat down a canal towing a float fished livebait behind him. Not only that, but he occasionally replaced the livebait with a plug – a float fished plug, no less!

I have tried a bit of trolled livebaiting and it works well, as all Norfolk anglers know today. On each water there is an optimum rowing speed giving a special action to the bait, and it is essential to discover what this is. The bait is lip-hooked and belly hooked, both very lightly, and a barrel lead is added above the trace in order to keep the bait down.

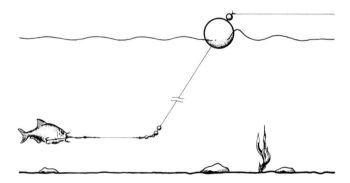

Rig used for trolled livebait or deadbait. Note that the speed of the boat introduces a small bow wave in front of the float, at which time it also wobbles from side to side: this is the ideal trolling speed.

The ideal speed seems to be when the float gives a characteristic wobble from side to side, and obviously the rowing speed varies with the depth, the current and the bait size. But there does seem to be an induced action for which one must strive. The basic tackle is, of course, the usual sliding float rig, minus paternoster link.

I have tried this technique from the banks of a fenland drain by a method I do not wish to enlarge upon at present – when I have it worked out I'll report on it fully. It does work; as does towing a float and plug. A sinking plug can be used and of necessity it can only dive so far, struggling to submerge the float. It reminds me of Richard Walker's float fished fly rigs (which I have also used successfully). Trolled livebaiting could be more widely used, as indeed could trolled deadbaiting using floats. If we did more boat fishing in this country I'm sure they would be.

I have not covered in this chapter every aspect of livebaiting. But I have covered what I regard as fundamental, and other lesser matters will be mentioned in context elsewhere in the tome.

CHAPTER FOUR

Chasing pike

An inexorable logic being one of my strong points, the deadbait and livebait chapters, dealing with increasingly active hunting methods adopted by the pike, should naturally be followed by a chapter on the most active of methods, that of lure fishing or spinning. I make no apology for the ambiguous chapter title for, in truth, the spinning angler is chasing pike, and he is chasing pike that are at their most active in hunting down anything that moves.

There are a few fundamentals to clear up before we get any further. Firstly, the matter of my own experience. I have lure fished for pike longer than I have used any other method, and have caught many, many good pike. I still lure fish extensively wherever I go piking and I still catch plenty of fish, summer and winter. But I have only once topped 20 lb on lures; a 23 lb fish that fell to a yellow, 4 in. Gudebrod Sniper on a tiny fenland drain.* That fish, and a 14-pounder the same day, was instructive in itself. Normally I fish this drain by dropping the lure beneath the rushes on the far bank. Most of the pike hang out within two feet of that bank. But weed cutting had been done and my own bank had rafts, each some three feet wide and a few feet long, scattered along the edge at intervals. The water beneath them was about one-foot deep, just enough to take the deep slung belly of a 20-pounder! *My* 20-pounder ghosted out from only a yard or two away (I was casting from between two of the rafts), hit the plug when it was only three feet from the rod tip and continued accelerating, half in and half out of the water, till it hit the rushes on the far bank. My rod was a six-foot glass wand and if I'd had the spinning handles of the reel near any bodily parts at the time of the take, they'd have sawed a deep hole!

---

*To which I added a further three in late 1985!

I wouldn't have caught that pike had my approach-work been anything other than stealthy. After all, I'd spent several minutes standing there and for all that time she wasn't nine feet away. But it *is* my only 20-pounder on lure and this brings me to the first home truth that lure fisherman must face up to; lure fishing, exciting, interesting, enjoyable though it is, is *not* as effective in piking as deadbaiting and livebaiting, not by a long way. So you lure fish because you love it. This is not to say you don't catch a lot of fish, for on several occasions I've had more than twenty-five in half a day's fishing.

What is spinning?

The question of terminology is a vexing one. Surely a lure fisherman is a man who fishes for trout? Well, the term is also used to describe those anglers who throw spinners, spoons, plugs, jigs, perks and feathers at predatory fish. Personally I tend to refer to it all as spinning, and this I believe is what U.K. anglers have always done, only using terms like plug fishing when they wish to be more specific. So that's what I'll do from now on. When I wish to be specific I'll use a specific term. Within spinning I like to include spun naturals and wobbled naturals, and I'll say a little about these towards the end of the chapter.

Sport-fishing

Spinning is *not* more sporting than other methods. This is an old wives' tale put about by anglers too lazy to partake in bait fishing and who needed an excuse for using what they knew in their hearts was an inferior method of angling. Only the angler is sporting, or otherwise, not the method he employs (unless that method is a fish destroyer such as nets, explosives, poisons, set lines etc., in which case it isn't angling anyway).

Spinning is not really popular in the U.K., so if you take it up you'll soon find yourself breaking new ground. In the U.S.A. and many other parts of the world – Europe, Scandinavia and Australia especially – it *is* popular and for this reason they have an enormous choice of lures compared to the U.K. If spinning were popular in the U.K. *we'd* have the choice of lures too, and two books on the subject by myself and Ken Whitehead (*Plugs and Plug Fishing* and *Spinners, Spoons and Wobbled Baits*: pubd. A & C Black) would have sold as many copies as *Fishing for Big Pike*. Certainly they cover the subject in depth and detail. In this country things go in phases, usually propagated by a guru or two. In my early days it was the legendary Fred Wagstaffe and his partner Bob Reynolds. Today it is Gordon Burton and others. We are, happily, in a lure craze phase at the moment! One indication of this is suggested by the way tackle firms are quickly trying to get some good lures in their stocks. I ought to say at this stage that any enterprising angler can write off to the American manufacturers for their catalogues and order his own. Of course, they are expensive, but the old adage of the more you have the less you lose is very, very true.

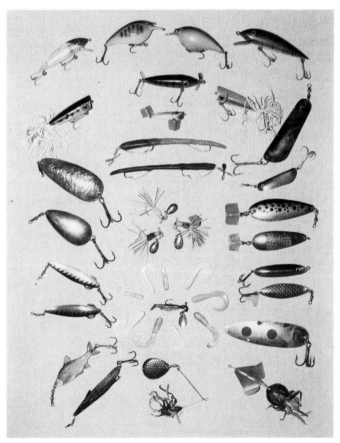

This exemplifies the great variety of artificial lures available to the present day spinning enthusiast. All the lures illustrated are *good* pike lures, especially that at the centre of the bottom row.

When to lure fish

What about *when* to fish lures? Well it's all very simple, unlike most angling matters. Summer is the time for lure fishing, up to and including earliest October. By November the fish are getting reluctant to chase, and through the winter it's a slow game. That doesn't stop me doing it, because I like it. But face facts – lures and success really only go together when the water is warm. Every keen spinning man has waters, and swims on waters, that fish well even in winter, so that he knows where to go and what to try. My own experience with respect to conditions is that if the barometer is rising or high, then pike are more likely to hunt actively. And those good winter lure swims also fish better in summer! I think, on balance, that wobbled naturals or spun naturals are a shade better than artificials and their use enables one to bridge the gap of autumn into winter because they retain their effectiveness a little longer.

As I have mentioned cold weather let's try to knock on the head another silly story, namely, that spinning in winter keeps you warm. What absolute balderdash! The easiest way to get cold in winter, especially cold hands, is to go spinning. The winter spinner is only warmed when he walks a long way without stopping. When he *does*

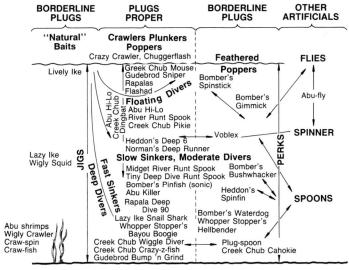

Classification-cum-mode-of-operation of plugs, spoons and spinners.
(After Rickards & Whitehead, 1976)

stop, and fishes, he's likely to catch a chill as any athlete could tell him. This fact doesn't stop people without any experience stating the opposite view – and frequently. You'll even find the same idiotic statement in an article under my name in a Marshal Cavendish partwork series – nothing to do with me, of course, but the editor inserted it because he thought it was needed! I even saw an article in a Sunday newspaper by the experienced game fisherman, Brian Clark, claiming the same thing; perhaps the editor worked a flanker on him too. If you want to keep warm spinning in winter, then do it in small bursts, dress up very, very carefully, and even indulge in spinning whilst sitting on a chair out of the wind! There's no hurry, remember, because the pike's certainly in no hurry when he's cold.

John Watson summer piking on the Norfolk Broads. This is the time when artificial can be as good as, or better than, natural baits.

Rod to use

You may think I'm skirting around the subject a little, but this is not so. It's as well to get the basics correct before wasting time firing plugs to far horizons whilst big pike yawn on the bottom as missiles whiz ineffectively overhead. What sort of rod do we need? Today it doesn't matter a great deal because the era of carbon fibre is with us. Rods used to be short for spinning because you had to hold them all day and any reduction in weight was welcome. You can hold an eleven-foot fast taper carbon pike rod all day without tiring, so you might just as well do so. My own experience is that it is unusual to be unable to wangle a long rod in confined circumstances. Usually you can manage quite well, and there are distinct advantages in a longish rod, such as the retrieve position of the bait relative to the angler. Should a pike follow you to the bankside, and your rod tip is eleven feet down the bank, then *you* are at least eleven feet away from the pike and you can crouch slowly without being seen. Incidentally, should this happen to you (and it will, often) you have two distinct choices of action depending upon whether you have attached a sinking artificial or a floating one. If it's a sinker you *must* be bold – speed up the retrieve even if it means running the wire trace into your end ring! If it's a floater, *stop* the retrieve immediately and let it float for about 10 – 20 seconds – then twitch it gently. You'll be staggered at the response of the pike; sometimes they couldn't have hit it more savagely if they'd been using a shillelagh.

Long rods also have clear advantages when fishing most banksides in the U.K., because nearly all banksides have sedgy margins over which you can reach more easily. Having said all that, I do use short rods quite often, down to five feet or so in length, because I enjoy doing so. My line and terminal gear is always strong so I have no worries on that score (see below). And my spinning rods, long or short, are usually telescopic. I have them made up complete with reel and line threaded through the rings, trace and first lure already attached. It takes but moments to start fishing, and if you do have to walk, the whole lot can be reeled up small in the twinkling of an eye. In winter I always carry such a rod *inside* my rucksack, whilst in summer I have a special rucksack as I shall explain in a later section.

Reels for spinning

Let me say at the outset that I've done the whole thing – centrepins, multipliers, and fixed spools. I don't use centrepins for spinning now, but I do use the other two types. I'd given up multipliers at one stage but came across an old left hand wind Abu and then Ryobi brought out a series of superb, left hand wind carbon multipliers (of which I bought myself two). Fixed spool reels, especially the small ones, do all that you can ask, but personally I get a lot of pleasure out of the multiplier. With today's magnetic brakes it really is a little difficult to get oneself into a pig's ear of a mess – unless you try to be too clever and have all nuts and washers hanging loose! I remember one nice day last winter, on the Relief Channel, taking fish after fish on the tiniest of the Ryobis coupled with a three inch Toby spoon – nothing big but consistent sport nevertheless.

I keep mentioning left hand wind multipliers, and you may well wonder at the repetition. Well, believe it or not, it's like this . . . most multipliers in the world are manufactured for left-handed anglers (i.e. they have the reel handles *on the right*), whereas most fixed spool reels can be adapted to either left hand or right hand use. A few, such as the Ryobi ones, cater for the right-handed angler and this can be very important. Let me explain. Using a *proper* multiplier you hold the rod with your right hand, cast, and pick up the line *immediately* with the left hand in control of the reel handles (*on the left*). To do it improperly you have to move the rod over to the *left* hand so you can take up the handles with the rod hand. Crazy? Of course it is. If you are right-handed insist on a left hand wind reel or tell the dealer that you'll buy someone else's brand of fixed spool reel (from another shop!).

Terminal rigs and line

Several of my friends never use line less than 15 lb b.s. for their piking, especially lure fishing where they may go up to 18 lb or 20 lb. I have no real logical argument to combat this and I, quite irrationally, use 12 lb b.s. Sylcast (dark coloured) or Platil. Sometimes I use 15 lb b.s. Sylcast (dark coloured) when I'm really worried! I think if you are on waters where the pike *frequently* run over 25 lb then I'm sure my friends are correct. More especially is this true when afloat or when fishing badly reeded margins. I use nylon monofilament and can at present see no point in using anything else.

Always, but always, use a wire trace, of some 6 – 10 inches length. Again, if it's big pike country then use the longer trace. Lure caught pike do roll on the trace and there's more than a chance their teeth will fetch up against nylon – and a 25-pounder could totally engulf a 6 inch trace. You will occasionally come across anglers who tie their lures direct to the reel line. They should be thrown in.

The wire to use is one of the cabled wires now readily available, such as Tidemaster, Steelstrand, Alasticum, P.D.Q. and so on. Most of them are good, but I personally avoid plastic-covered wire because it soon shreds off with the action of the pike's teeth (proving my earlier point, of course!) and it looks unsightly. You need a small swivel at one end and a link swivel at the other. Link swivels eventually weaken in the safety pin portion, but it is a slow process and you can discard them in ample time (the trace may well wear out or kink before that happens). Only once in my life have I had a swivel break, so they at least are reliable.

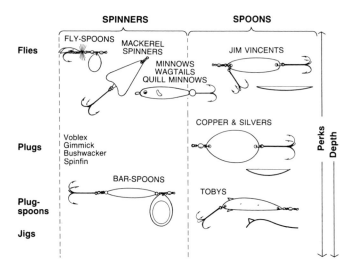

Classification of spinners and spoons.
(After Rickards & Whitehead, 1977)

Use of spinners can kink the line, although spoons and plugs are usually safe enough. Anti-kink vanes or leads always seem to me to be designed to fall off the line at the slightest provocation. Make sure that one end is firmly attached to your trace wire swivel, then knot your line to the anti-kink device swivel. Under no circumstances attach anything at all to a split ring (what splits apart to go on will split apart to come off!). If an anti-kink device terminates in split rings, and you cannot take them off, then attach a swivel to them because metal on metal is less dangerous than nylon on metal.

Lure bags etc.

From the foregoing you might well think we were all ready for the off! Not so. A little later I shall outline what lures you need and why, but for the moment you need to know where and how to carry them – especially if you are very rich and have a lot, or are very handy and have made a lot.

When boat fishing, all is made relatively simple because there are numerous commercial varieties of plastic lure boxes taking anything from five or six to about a hundred or so. You cannot carry the larger versions of such boxes when bank fishing. Even in a boat there *are* improved ways of doing things. One can, for example, hang a piece of foambacked nylon carpet over the gunwale! Lures can be hung on this with no fear for their safety and a large selection can be readily and visibly to hand. However, I would strongly advise you not to trip and fall on such a lure display for I doubt whether you'd ever get off . . . Another trick is the patent individual, transparent lure separator – simply a row of plastic bottles cut in half and held in a row with hessian or canvas webbing. String it along the gunwale and all is permanently revealed.

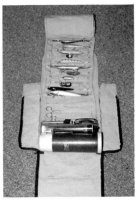

The roll-up lure holdall designed by the author to accommodate all one needs for a day's lure fishing: the lures are easily accessible and remain untangled.

On the bank I use the lure bag of my own design, as illustrated. The idea of this bag is self-evident; almost everything you need for the day goes in the one bag, so that when wandering along the bank you have a rod in one hand and a net in the other. All the rest, be it food, drink, camera, light anorak, overtrousers, forceps, weighing bag and balance, is in the bag on your back. But, more importantly, the lure roll, which is designed to keep all lures separate, is above all the miscellaneous junk so that upon opening the bag you have before your eyes a full choice of lures. It works well, and at the end of the day the telescopic rod fits in, as does the landing net, so you simply walk back using the landing net pole as a walking stick!

All this ingenious design on my part would be entirely – or largely – unnecessary if the tackle trade got its act together and issued *all* spinners, spoons and plugs *without* hooks. Either the lures would have standard links attached or the treble hooks would have them. Either would do. I'm sure the trade would then sell far more plugs *and* trebles; and anglers could pack their pockets with lure bodies whilst keeping a quantity of hooks in a small tin. Too much to ask, of course!

There is one other way round the nasty problem of enormous tangled masses of spinners and spoons and plugs, and that is to fit treble guards on all the trebles. To do the job fully a keen lure fisherman would need several hundred! They do work, however, especially the latest version marketed by Ryobi Masterline. I've used such things, on and off (usually off) for almost fifteen years, but old versions did have a habit of falling off some trebles, or failing to fit, or worse, fitting dangerously stiffly. The new versions are much more flexible in every sense of the word.

First steps . . .

You'll be surprised to learn that we're all ready to go spinning! One thing you'll be advised to do time and again is to spin 'around the clock', that is, before moving on, cover all the water in a series of casts, each at a slightly different angle. Don't do it. Try to work out, in each swim, where the fish is most likely to be, then cast to catch it. The above 'traditional' method is boring, time-consuming and I think it confuses the pike! Any pike in the vicinity *knows* your lure has hit the water – that's what he's in business for. If your lure is small, as it should be to start with, it may take him some time to wake up to it, and he may creep slowly across to have a look. But if it's a whacking great lure it may frighten him straight off. Whatever the circumstances he'll know it's there, make no mistake. For this very reason the first couple of casts in a swim are often crucial. So do not waste too long in a swim unless you feel that a different lure is called for, or persistence – but do not unthinkingly stay there until you start yawning.

It is often exceedingly difficult to decide whether to fish up top or go down below. But two widely applicable guidelines will help a little. One is that your retrieve should always be as slow and steady as you can make it, and if you are fishing below the surface it should always be as deep as you can fish it. There are exceptions, of course, but you learn to try them in appropriate circumstances. Secondly, always use a small lure if you can, at least to begin with, and as a general rule opt for a bright lure under dull conditions and a dull lure under bright conditions. These tricks give you a basic *modus operandi* and you can then ring the changes according to a basic pattern. This way you learn. The chuck-and-chance it methods teach you little, even if you are lucky.

Which lure?

I'm going to leave spinning from boats until the boat fishing chapter (Chapter Seven) because it really is one of the prime boat fishing skills. Now, I'd like to deal with the choice of lure. The two tables/figures really do have an awful lot condensed into them. The names of lures on them are, for example, very good lures that I would always have with me. The illustrations also roughly depict how and where to fish the lures. It will be obvious to you from the preceding section that I have already introduced a number of variables: colour, type, size, for example. A few minutes' calculation will quickly reveal that to cover all eventualities you need *hundreds* of lures. It isn't necessary of course, but how do we sensibly restrict the total to a few dozen?

Look at the classifications first of all. The vast bulk of good plugs are the floating divers, so fifteen or so different sizes and colours will cover most circumstances. You don't *really* need deep divers in fact, because you can fish a floater on a paternoster link! Spoons come in basically three types, what I call the Jim Vincent (or Norfolk) spoon, the things like eggs that I call Copper and Silvers, and the slim Jim concave-convex spoons like Toby spoons. Again you need perhaps three or four of each in your bag, in different sizes and colours. There really is no general need to have every colour in every size for every spoon, unless you wish to do so in your main lure box back in the car or in the tackle shed. Spinners again come in very few basic kinds: the (so-called) bar-spoon; the mackerel type; and the minnows (quill, metal or wood). These tend to be used at close range, quietly, and *slowly*. Some do, however, cast to prodigious distances and yet can be fished quite shallowly, either slow or fast.

In waters with thick weed which either doesn't quite reach the surface or does so in patches, then I tend to use a surface crawler like the Crazy Crawler, or a mackerel spinner fished very shallow. Should there be deepish holes amongst weed beds then I go for floating divers such as the Big S or similar plugs. Spoons I like to fish in weed-free areas, and at great depth I prefer them to plugs and spinners. A good place for a shallow-fished, big Jim Vincent, or a very large, floating, jointed plug, is in a big wave on shallow water, such as in a good south-westerly on the Norfolk Broads.

CHAPTER FIVE

Tackles and techniques

A useful measure of advances in any subject is the extent to which the subject has become simplified. During the last decade both tackle and techniques have been simplified considerably, in the latter case because we now have a much better understanding of what really works, and why. Tackle has improved partly because of design changes and partly because of materials changes. To this day I would maintain that rods are the least important of the rod-reel-line-hook combination. In fact if you reversed that order you'd have the hierarchy about right. But I'll discuss rods first because it may be easier nowadays to do this.

Rods

I still have several glass, and cane rods, such as the Oliver's stepped up carp, which I use with enjoyment. But almost exclusively now I use carbon rods. During the last few years the number of rods has been reduced from a huge variety and continuous spectrum into two basic types, namely fast (or tip) action and slow (or through) action. It was becoming clear in the 1960s that the through action rod would throw a big deadbait a long way – such as a whole herring, half a frozen mackerel, or a livebait and paternoster lead. The fast action rods were good for firing concentrated, reasonably heavy weights a long way – say, a 2–4 oz lead with a small bait. This division into two basic types of rod has continued with carbon. I use John Watson's slow action, twelve-foot rod made by Bruce and Walker, and my own fast action, eleven-foot rod made by East Anglian Rod Company.

It will be noticed immediately that the rods are longer than in the past, when ten-foot rods were more usual. This reflects use of the lighter and stronger carbon material in the blanks. The carbon rods are to my mind more versatile than glass and they certainly cast further and are lighter to use. So my two rods cover 95 per cent of my piking. In fact, I'd be happy to use either for all my piking if I was forced to do so. Actually I do use other rods: cane rods, short rods, and so on as the fancy takes me. But my bank equipment for deadbaiting, livebaiting and spinning are the Watson and Rickards rods.

Rod fittings

Rod fittings have largely changed for the better. Fuji or similar rings are used throughout and the single leg variety is quite suitable on pike rods, adding almost nothing to the weight of the rod. Handles often come in the new black, spongy material. It is easy on the eye, comfortable, but I like it less than cork. Reel seatings need to be more complicated because the composition material is more compressible than cork – simple sleeves compress the material and during playing may allow the reel to shift position. My own E.A.R. rods have a slotted sleeve reel seating which does away with the problem, but now the sleeves look ugly! Cork is better, but from the manufacturers' point of view is less easy to deal with.

The Fuji-type of ring makes for less resistance on the cast and is, therefore, better in this sense also. But ring spacing is a problem, even though it need not be. There has been a tendency, stemming from the world of carp fishing, to reduce considerably the number of rings on a rod, in some cases down to two or three plus the tip ring. My own Black Eleven has only six rings in total. It certainly seems to aid casting but I distinctly sense more resistance in playing fish than there should be. In retrospect I think eight rings is about correct. My Watson rod is, if anything, over-ringed. However, all this is a relatively small matter and perhaps one of personal feeling. What is agreed widely is that the relatively dull black rods and fittings are aesthetically a distinct advance on previous rods. They *do* look good and are a pleasure to use.

Reels

When it comes to reels I am in a similar position to that with respect to rods. I use centrepins when I feel like a change. I use left hand wind multipliers made by Ryobi because they are superb for lure fishing. But mostly I use Mitchel and Ryobi fixed spool reels. My latest and best is the Ryobi Graphite ML3.5, a superb reel for piking. It is not dissimilar to Shakespeare's excellent Sigma Graphite, but I reserve that for roach fishing so have no first-hand knowledge of how it measures up to piking. Increasingly it seems that modern reels are of the skirted variety. I suppose they really are necessary but I prefer the look of the old sort.

A further word about left hand wind multipliers. I know many anglers, right-handed anglers, who use right hand wind multipliers. After casting they pass the rod from the right to the left hand so that they play the fish with their poorest arm, just to enable them to use their right hand on the reel handles! Crazy, ugly, and inefficient. Why not left-hand wind? Because by and large the manufacturers do not make them. In fact for freshwater fishing I think only Ryobi do them. Abu used to make one, an excellent reel which I use regularly, but unlike the Ryobi it isn't lightweight and in carbon.

Slipping clutches on reels are in order of magnitude better than they were ten years ago, yet when I take them apart they seem the same. Personally I don't like those situated at the rear of the reel, but it seems everyone else does . . . ! Handles are mostly flat, which makes them convenient for cold fingers in winter – round handles were exceedingly difficult to grip when you had no feeling in your finger ends.

Lines

I am extremely fussy about lines, not so much the make, but the quality, breaking strain and lack of flaws. I constantly run my fingers over nylon monofil searching for kinks and the fraying which may indicate a grooved or cracked rod ring. I do not so much mind fish shedding the hooks during playing, nor do I mind missing on the strike, but I really hate getting snapped up. The first two 'happenings' can occur through no fault of your own, but to get snapped up means there's only one person to blame, namely yourself. Nylon monofil is of superb quality these days, though some of it could have less shine, be of better colour, and be more supple, and there is no doubt in my mind that it can go 'off' overnight, but generally there are few problems. Also available are plaited nylon, terylene and courlene lines, lead-cored lines, fly lines and so on. It hardly matters which is used provided the angler constantly watches for flaws, and regularly tests the breaking strain by, at the very least, giving it a good tug.

The breaking strains I normally employ for big pike are 9 – 15 lb, usually 11 lb, but if a great deal of casting is done a short shock leader of up to 20 – 25 lb can be used. Or, if fishing amongst sunken trees one might possibly wish to go up to over 20 lb. The pike angler should never be ashamed of using strong lines to suit particular circumstances, or even his own inability. There really is no merit at all in leaving pike swimming around with hooks in their jaws, in spite of the mutterings of some writers who seem to like the idea of having 'breaking-strain records'. This sort of thing makes me wonder whether the philosophical advances of the last twenty years have actually got through to some people.

I used to fish a lot with a chap we called Sharkbait Robbo. He always used enormous baits and lines of up to 60 lb breaking strain for piking. His idea was that if he ever did latch on to a 40-pounder then it was '. . . . coming out, mate, it's coming out'. He also knew that he attended his lines very poorly, and calculated that even with a bad flaw a 60 lb line could hardly fail below 20 lb b.s. Everything happened to this chap, mostly through his own doing, but I once witnessed a bizarre scene on the Market Weighton canal in East Yorkshire, where he was more or less blameless as far as I could judge.

Sharkbait was fishing the rough west bank down towards the Foulness mouth and was trotting the stream with a small livebait attached by sea hooks to a cable-like trace and hence to 60 lb b.s. line. The line did not float, and the description 'trotting the stream' does not quite fit the activity. On the east bank of this narrow canal, trotting along more or less level with Sharkbait, was young Prask, another member of a somewhat fiendish specimen group. Prask got a run on his bream livebait, fished to 8 lb b.s. line, and promptly told the world about it. Not to be outdone, Sharkbait also declared a run about ten seconds later. After a while it became clear that Prask and Sharkbait were pulling not so much into a fish, but more against each other, and when a fish surfaced in the middle of the canal it was downright obvious that the pike had taken both their livebaits. With loud roars, the modern equivalent of which would be 'Get knotted, Prask!' Robbo proceeded to heave with all his might towards the west bank, and Prask proceeded to heave with all his might towards the east bank. Those of us watching, quite apart from trying to contain ourselves on the bank, placed our bets on Prask, for we knew the age of the 60 lb b.s. line. We won our bets, and our bank (for the rest of us were on the east bank) gained a huge float and some huge hooks, as well as a somewhat bewildered 5 lb pike. I do not think there are any morals to be culled from that episode.

The actual brands of line I use are Sylcast (dark brown) and Platil. I think I prefer the Sylcast because of the colour. It is also rounder and maybe casts a little better than the Platil, which I cannot otherwise fault. If you are using half blood knots then Sylcast will take up to seven turns and still make a real knot, whereas Platil takes only up to five turns, at least in the 11 – 12 lb b.s. lines that I use. Maxima is a good line too, but it just happened that when I wanted a bulk spool or two I couldn't get them so switched over to Sylcast.

Hooks

What a minefield of fetishes this subject is! I use Ryobi's Eagle Claw and various hooks by Partridge. Treble sizes are 10 – 6, except on lures when it may be necessary to go much larger, and on wobbled deadbaits when size 4 wouldn't come amiss on occasions. There are other good makes and there has been a clear improvement in quality in recent years. Eyes are smaller, barbs are smaller, and the wire is strong. (Too thick in some styles, perhaps?) You can also use semi-barbless and barbless hooks. The use of these latter is a matter of personal choice. I think myself that it is wrong to use barbless hooks, and I deplore the so-called codes of conduct of the N.A.C. which recommend use of them (admittedly 'where possible'). The idea of the semi-barbless hook is that the hook which goes into the bait has a barb. Why? Because it would fall out without it, that's why! And that's why the hook going into the pike should have a barb. However, I'll make few friends by stating this so let's leave it as a matter of personal choice. The ease-of-unhooking argument doesn't impress me a great deal I'm afraid.

Other tackle

Before going on to describe the best techniques of piking I want to spend a little time on miscellaneous tackle simply because it is so important to success. My own 'total pack' of equipment comprises a large rucksack, a rod holdall of my own design, and sometimes a bait bucket. It's efficient and it's compact. Sometimes it becomes too heavy! This is because I allow items to accumulate and do not pare back the load often enough. After all, you only need a couple of spare floats for a trip, not a dozen; half a dozen lures will do if you are basically bait fishing; a few extra leads are all that are normally needed.

However, I do carry a camera and flash, and binoculars for bird and bailiff watching. One pocket in the rucksack has a mass of stuff, including PVA tape and string, line floatant, spare vanes for E.T. floats, drifter floats, licences, polythene bags, string, screwdriver, spare floats, spare hooks (swivels and wire too). As a general rule I carry one spare reel and a couple of spare spools full to the brim with Sylcast 12 lb b.s. monofil. A couple of foam rubbers are at the back of the bag so that when walking they are next to my back. A pair of over-trousers is at the bottom of the bag. Unhooking equipment and leads are in a front pocket, and I also carry a few bends of stiff wire in case I need to stake out a gassed-up pike. All this stuff fails to fill the bag so I have room for food, flasks, and deadbaits, with the net and chair strapped to the outside. Once the rucksack is on my back an upstanding piece of metal tube locates the strap of my holdall so that I have two hands free whilst walking. Finally, I have a bigger rucksack if I want to carry my brolly camp with me!

A basic rig of quality

My idea in this section is not to discuss details of hook rigs because I have illustrated and described these elsewhere in the book, but to outline a first-class basic rig and then to demonstrate how it can quickly be varied to cover almost all angling eventualities in piking.

The first thing I have on the line is a stop knot. After years of trying various materials I now use 6 lb b.s. monofil almost exclusively. The only danger with it is that overtightening can weaken the line. Experience teaches one how to have it not too tight and not too slack so that it slips too easily on the line. When I'm spinning I leave the stop knot on the line, for the click of it going through the tip ring tells me exactly how far from the bank the lure is, and at night especially that is useful.

Next on the line I thread a plastic bead which has a diameter of about 3 – 4 mm, and a hole through the middle to take 15 lb b.s. monofil as a tight fit. After the bead on goes a sliding float, usually today perfectly circular, cork, and with a diameter of half an inch (for sunken float fishing) or 1½ – 2 inches. The principle is that the stop knot stops the bead and the bead stops the float. This allows the float to have quite a sizeable hole through its middle so that it slides on the line very freely. Clearly, the float is easy enough to remove should one wish to revert quickly to ledgering.

Below the float is a swan shot (or substitute equivalent). A ledger stop would do just as well. If I am deadbaiting, the shot goes right against the trace swivel which follows next in setting up the tackle. If I am livebaiting, the shot goes about two feet up the line from the trace. The purpose behind this is simply to prevent the livebait swimming upwards and hanging the hooks on the stop shot – with a paternoster rig in use this cannot happen if the stop shot is a couple of feet up the line.

Then comes the trace and bait. So far you can see that there is little difference between deadbaiting and free drift livebaiting, except for the position of the stop shot. In the event of wishing to paternoster, a link of lighter line is tied to the bottom ring of the trace swivel and a lead is attached at the other end of the link. The length can be varied to suit the circumstances but my standard is to try to fish the livebait about one to two feet off the bottom, sometimes shallower, and have a paternoster link, deeper (or shallower) as appropriate, and move the stop shot away from the trace swivel. In all, it takes less than thirty seconds! For ledgering or floatless paternostering you need to retie a knot after removing the float – again, hardly a time-consuming

The basic stop knot, bead and sliding float rig which is now almost universal amongst float-using pike anglers.

Avoid tangled and kinked wire traces by making a trace holder. Commercial models are now readily available.

matter. Drifter floats, sunken paternoster floats, heavy sliding leads, can all be added or substracted in a matter of a few seconds. If I change to spinning all I do is to drop the float down to the stop and then slip the whole lot (except bead and stop knot) into the rucksack, tie on my wire trace and all is ready again.

You can see how the rig really does equip me for almost all my piking. The drifter rig line will, of course, have a floatant on it. I usually keep this spool separate because although the other techniques can also be used with a floating line there are difficulties sometimes when the wind is bad. Above all, I would raise two further points about this versatile rig: 1. It is highly efficient, as witnessed by well over 900 double figure pike I have had fall to it; 2. it is no compromise rig in any sense, but the one I choose as the *best* rig for most circumstances.

In what circumstances would I vary it? Well, if I was drifting a large frozen mackerel out over deep water I'd replace the snap tackle with a Dave Steuart multihook rig. Were I using suspended sprat I might use a single large hook. Otherwise it is simply a question of varying the depth, to increase or decrease drag; the paternoster link length to restrict or give more freedom to the bait; the weight itself to give more distance or to hold bottom in different flow regimes; possibly the float itself to achieve different effects (of visibility, carrying capacity) and so on. It is unusual to find this set-up inadequate but I do occasionally begin to worry when I see or read of the rigs used by some anglers – until I ask myself *why* are they doing such a complicated thing. Then I remember, often, that I'd done it myself, years ago.

I have only briefly mentioned tangling, and that in connection with livebaits. However, long range ledgering with big sliding leads does cause tangles. There are several anti-tangle rigs both on the market and

Author's now standard hooking arrangement for half (and whole) deadbaits. The right-hand hook (as shown) is a freely sliding Ryder hook. The trebles rarely exceed size 6. With whole baits the hooks are kept in the same to-the-rear-of-the-bait position.

as designed by individual anglers. They all work quite well and, just occasionally, I find myself using them. The simplest way of avoiding tangles is to add an extra swivel and short length of line somewhere in the tackle line-up. Thus, above the trace swivel have another foot of line (or wire, or plastic tube over line) then another swivel just below the sliding lead. For some reason which escapes me this rig is less prone to flip-back and tangling. Another trick is to trail the fingers on the spool a second or so before the bait hits the water. This allows the bait to travel ahead of the lead, but it pays *to watch that it has done so*. If in doubt, retrieve it.

A simple, cheap rig which, when carefully arranged, will indicate slack line bites as well as straight pulls.

I think it is clear from the foregoing that what I do *not* do is set up a completely different rig for each type of water or technique in use. In fact all that is needed in most circumstances is a very slight adjustment, subtraction, or addition to the tackle system. And in claiming that, it shouldn't be forgotten that I fish a great variety of waters for pike: fast and slow; shallow and deep; clean or snaggy; muddy or rocky, and so on. The accompanying figures reinforce my claim. The one area where I *do* have to change is in the sphere of distance fishing, recently re-developed. This I wish to consider next.

CHAPTER SIX

Target horizon

The easiest way to reach the far horizon is to use a boat. Unfortunately for us they are banned on many of our waters so I'll deal with these rather special circumstances in the next chapter. In the past, pikers tended to fish the near banks. In truth, the tackle in use did not lend itself to much else. In recent years, however, there has been a tendency to fish as far away as possible, and not without good reason. I learnt, even in the days when pike anglers were thin on the banks, that many pike *were* well offshore, or in mid-river, and not as the pundits would have it, close to the banks. Here was a case of tackle limitations giving rise to an incorrect conclusion. Boat anglers must always have known that the pike can be in the middle of the lake, even when bank fishing is banned! Today there is an increased need for distance fishing related to the crowds on the bank, for pike which naturally lived within a comfortable cast have surely tended to leave the shore, having been caught a couple of times.

How far? When I did the first edition I wrote of casting half mackerel 100 yards on a slow, powerful rod like the Oliver's stepped up carp rod; or casting a *small* live or deadbait similar distances using a fast action rod and heavy lead. That's still good distance fishing for most circumstances, and if you can do it you'll not miss much piking. Using the latest sea angling techniques it is, however, now possible to chuck the baits (especially small baits) in excess of 150 yards. Although you do not need a heavy reel line for this you do need a strong shock leader (say 18 or 20 lb b.s.) and a heavy lead (say 3 – 5 oz). The bait can be tied with PVA to a ledger stop halfway down the lead link, so that all is streamlined on the cast, the lead being the terminal element. But we really ought to try the latest sea anglers' bait capsules which release the bait from a lead cored container upon impact with the water! I haven't tried one as I write but only because I do not seem to be able to obtain one. The modern carbon rods do mean that all these distances can be achieved much more easily than in the past and it is reassuring to see that both slow and fast carbons are available – indeed, I have both myself, the John Watson slow action, twelve-footer, and my own design fast action, eleven-footer.

Perhaps I should briefly footnote those remarks. In addition to the above tackle you do need a modicum of commonsense. Do choose the right weight for the rod. Do get the rig streamlined. Make sure that the spool lip is full to the brim and that all knots are smoothly made and positioned on the spool so that there is no snatching on casting. If the lead is on a running swivel then its weight hardly matters; and if it is fixed I suspect it doesn't! When I used to think that I abhorred any lead over half an ounce weight . . . Don't abandon floats too readily. When used as a sunken float they can be quite small, so as not to affect distance much, and they do have the advantage of helping to keep the line out of snags on the bottom.

But the last few years have seen other ways of achieving prodigious distances. I personally believe that to go over 300 yards is probably wrong, tempting though it must be on some occasions. At 250 yards I have had the greatest difficulty contacting the pike on the strike! Perhaps 150 – 250 yards is the range to aim for. Essentially, there are four ways of doing this.

The contemplative man's recreation: viewing the vastness of Loch Lomond, armed with a four-inch Sniper plug.

Malcolm Bannister, 1986 Secretary of the Pike Anglers' Club, conquers the vastness of Loch Lomond with this big twenty-pounder.

Balloons

You need a balloon which, when inflated, has a diameter of about one foot or more. A paper clip is attached to the top swivel on the trace, and also to the knot on the balloon. I also wrap PVA around the balloon knot and clip because otherwise there is a tendency for the balloon to come off as you swing it out! You cannot cast, of course, and you must have a good wind close to your bank for that reason. If you have fifty yards of flat calm in front of you, then no amount of back wind will take out the balloon. Assuming it has gone out to where you need it the PVA will have dissolved and you can give a good strike to pull the clip off the balloon. The balloon then disappears across the lake and usually heads off across the countryside unless it impinges on a hedge. It could hardly be described as litter.

For this kind of angling it is advisable to use greased, floating line particularly if the bait is to be fished off the bottom. You can, of course, use a float in the normal way, and a paternoster rig too if the water near your bank is deeper than the length of the paternoster. If not, roll up the paternoster rig and PVA it to the swivel. It looks a bit of a bundle but it works well.

Colin Dyson drifter

This is the best ever of the wind catching drifters, which have, in fact, been around many years. But this one gets it absolutely right. The only drawback, and there's a way around that, is when the depth you wish to fish is twenty feet and water in front of you is ten feet deep for fifty yards! What you do is use a balloon in combination! Use PVA to tie balloon, float and trace swivel together in a big knot (which dissolves slowly) then cast it as far as you can. It will certainly go at least fifty yards before the PVA dissolves, and after that it doesn't matter because the drifter takes over. Floating line is used, as in ballooning, and I let the vagaries of the wind work the bait back and forth in big arcs. Then I let out a bit more line and off it goes again. Colin Dyson is one of the most experienced pikers in the land and he and his colleagues are to be congratulated in coming up with a system that really works and is nice to use. I've already gone over 20 lb on my own home-made float so I'm well pleased.

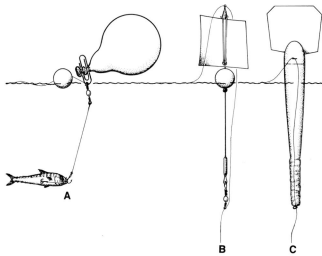

A

B   C

Three drifting systems which can get the tackle up to 250 yards. A, balloon used to tow out standard rig; the paper clip should be attached to the *knot* of the balloon so that it *does not catch* and then carefully tied in position with PVA tape or string; B, the Eddie Turner drifter system; C, the Colin Dyson drifter float.

E.T. rigs

These go so far so fast that they might well be extraterrestrial. They were invented by Eddie Turner and friends and do commercially what the Colin Dyson floats do. They have a very large vane and really do catch the wind at times. I use a lead at the end of the wire because a real howler has a tendency to blow them flat otherwise. Contrary to the literature I have not found the vane a nuisance on the retrieve when it's in the fixed, upright position, so that is how I now use it. Everything is fixed so that it doesn't fall off – I don't like losing vanes, especially as they sink! E.T. also came up with a good floatant grease which certainly seems a great deal better to me than my old Mucilin. Once again, by judicious use of PVA and a little jiggery pokery as in the preceding two sections, you can usually overcome most circumstances. I would echo many of E.T.'s comments, especially that one must keep a wary eye on the tackle all the time because it *is* so far away. It is also necessary to strike quickly because *immediate* bite indication is not always clear and it takes a while anyway to make contact. As the Colin Dyson rig, this is a beautiful invention. Of course it'll be used often when not necessary and I have already seen anglers struggling, under the wrong circumstances, to reach fifty yards with it. It would have been better to cast with normal tackle.

Radio controllers

This principle uses a radio controlled boat to take out the bait great distances. It has been used for some time by both carp and pike anglers – those that feel the expense is worth it. To some it may not justify the expense. It certainly works, according to those who have used it. I haven't myself, and the only time I saw someone trying he didn't have a great deal of success and looked like losing his boat, all £100 plus of it! I shouldn't have laughed, I know. I don't want to belittle the method. My good friend Jim Housden uses it with great success.

The Great Ouse, a deep, slow and wide river that provides its own unfathomable problems. From this water came the author's best fish of just over 32 lb.

CHAPTER SEVEN

Esox afloat

As in so many spheres, boat fishing has been transformed, even though we do not yet have many of those superb custom built anglers' boats that they use in the U.S.A. and in Scandinavia. The time will come, of course, but for the present we have moved on only from clinker-built wooden boats, of which I have considerable personal experience, to fibre glass. Having spent a great deal of time in boats supposedly designed for angling I could certainly design one now should someone ask me! There are two important factors in boating for pike that you must come to grips with immediately and these are shipshapeness, bordering on a fanatical tidiness, and safety. If you fish with a friend then teamwork can be vital, most especially in times of danger. In pike fishing these matters are more important than usual because you may well be in very exposed situations, and the amount of dangerous equipment lying about the boat – not to mention a porcupine of rods – is considerable. What I should like to do now is let Ray Webb take up these several themes before drawing everything together toward the end of the chapter, introducing a few new ideas.

'Having spent so much of my angling time over the last ten years afloat in a considerable variety of crafts, for it has not always been possible, or even desirable, to operate from my own in every circumstance, it has been easy for me to form a comprehensive idea of the advantages and disadvantages of boat angling, the situation where it so frequently wins hands down and the occasional one where it does not. Perhaps the first advantage to being afloat that became obvious immediately when I started fishing the Norfolk Broads, was the fact that it opened up so much water that would otherwise have been inaccessible because of excessive casting distances. Banks that were waterlogged, boggy, or fringed by a fifteen-yard margin of reeds two

This piratical gentleman, Gordon Burton, achieves more success than most when afloat, and especially on big waters.

or three feet high, or in many cases festooned with "Private Keep Out" notices, that made any approach from the landward side extremely hazardous were now within my reach. In those days the method in favour was livebaiting, fished intensively in one spot for a mere twenty minutes or so then up anchoring and on to another swim. By doing this a considerable area of water was covered in a day's fishing. This of course was the style adopted and publicised by Dennis Pye. His tremendous returns put him way out ahead in the history of pike fishing and absolutely in a class of his own. They were, however, only possible by tackling the waters involved from a boat; without one he could not have hoped for comparable results. Another point where the boat proved its worth was in the matter of studying the water, looking for likely swims prior to going out with the tackle set up for a serious attempt to catch fish. So much of the most promising water of the Upper Thurne area being clear and shallow, it was a common practice of Pye and others to spend a considerable amount of time quietly drifting the boat along, keeping an eye out for likely spots. Very often the pike themselves were spotted and the position carefully noted in readiness for the time when angling in earnest would begin. I myself on many occasions in the close season, have launched the old boat, *Tinca* by name after my other great favourite species, the tench, and have taken pencil and paper aboard and spent countless hours compiling maps showing depth contours, weed beds, snags, variations in the nature of the bottom etc., so recording information that has come in handy time and again; often long after the survey was carried out and the information obtained forgotten. Virtually all my work in this field however was carried out in water of far greater depth and colour than

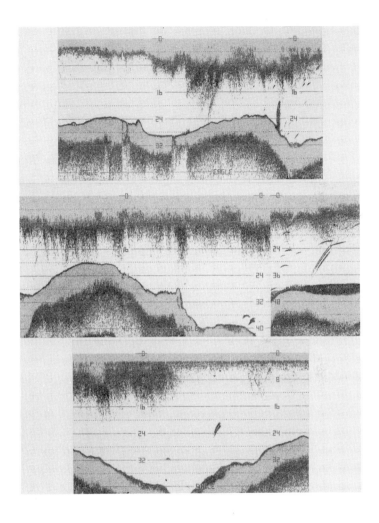

Echo sounders are a boon to the big water enthusiasts and a must for boat anglers. These print-outs came from a Lowrance echo sounder used by Colin Dyson and the author on Ardingly Reservoir in Sussex. The upper graph shows the irregular bottom contours and a sunken tree (near the 24-feet depth figure), below and to the right of which are several large fish. The middle graph shows big fish located just above 40 feet, and three fast-moving fish, as well as other large fish, between 36 and 24 feet. The cloudiness towards the top of each graph could be caused by algae or clay mineral (mud) particles, but groups of small fish can also be identified.

that of the Upper Thurne, so the job was done by employing a heavy
weight attached to a long cord, sounding the bottom in this fashion,
much the same as the naval men have done for centuries by swinging
the lead to guide their boats safely over shallow water. Pye of course
is strictly a livebaiting man, but Jim Vincent preferred to employ a 5
in spoon, a method where the regular casting and retrieving involved
inevitably means getting snagged up with some frequency, far more
so perhaps than with any other technique, and if operating on foot from
the bank, heavy tackle losses can become an expensive item. Out in
a boat, however, the chances of recovering hooked-up baits are greatly
improved; by moving directly over the snag and employing a gaff in
shallow water or some sort of drag on a stout cord in the deeps, the
tackle plus the obstruction itself can on many occasions be hauled up
to the surface. Very often, by working in this fashion, I have not only
retrieved my own bait but also a bonus in the shape of other lines,
swivels, anti-kink vanes and fold-over leads. Some of the more
formidable obstacles, if in a heavily fished location, can yield a bumper
harvest – and a very rich and worthwhile harvest in these inflationary
times, for the price of pike baits has soared in recent years, as indeed
have all costs of equipment. Another point where the man in the boat
scores heavily if spinning in clear water, is in his ability to actually see
his bait working from the moment it hits the water. He is able to observe
its action, the depth at which it is operating, and the amount of flash
it is emitting.

By being able to work in close to the pike and fish a fairly short line
all these things can be observed visually whereas the bank angler,
usually having to go in for extreme distance casting, can only work by
the feel of his tackle, a far less effective method of operation. It is
surprising how some spoons fish with a lively action in flowing water
but when transferred to a lake come in completely dead, needing
considerable modification with a pair of pliers before they are working
satisfactorily. One of the greatest thrills of all in pike fishing is to
actually see the fish dart out and take the lure, as can frequently happen
when afloat. I remember vividly one occasion, when after casting and
retrieving a 4 in blue and silver spoon time and time again through four
feet of clear, fast-running water without any sign of response, suddenly,
just as the bait was under the rod tip and about to be lifted clear of the
surface, a huge shape materialised, moved to the bait with astonishing
rapidity, just about drowned me with spray as it turned to race away
up and across the stream, and fought with tremendous power for some

considerable time before finishing up in the net. For sheer, breathtaking impact this style of fishing is in a class of its own.

There is more to it than mere enjoyment. By watching the take, making note of where the pike came from, what depth it took at, which way it went on being hooked and how it actually grabbed the lure in its mouth, it is possible to gain a lot of information which will prove of value. By moving the boat over to the spot where the fish came from for instance, a close inspection will often, after a number of captures have been made, see a pattern emerging as to the type of swim to look

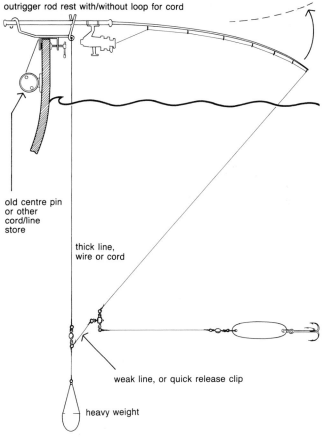

Downrigger system for trolling artificial or natural lures. A home-made version is shown, though sophisticated and expensive commercial versions are available.

for, so improving one's knowledge and prospects for future sport. One such examination after the taking of a superb pike of 28¼ lb caused me some astonishment for the fish had been lying quietly in a mere eighteen inches of water completely unperturbed by my drifting downstream to within ten yards of it before lowering the anchor, admittedly as quietly as possible, and then commencing casting and retrieving. Only two or three casts were made when the pike struck, missed, struck again, successfully this time and surged away downstream on the longest run I ever experienced with any fish. There must have been seventy or eighty yards of line ripped off the spool in double quick time before I succeeded in halting the initial rush. The fight continued at extreme long range for what seemed an eternity but was, I suppose, in fact some ten minutes long. From that day on I have never written off even the shallowest water as being incapable of holding outsize specimens, but thinking it over, the river was running high, fast and coloured at the time. It was in fact just fining down after a flood, otherwise perhaps a pike of his weight would hardly have been taken from quite so close to the bank.

Probably the biggest drawback of all to boat fishing is the danger involved, especially on the larger waters. In spite of all the warnings every year sees a number of fatal accidents many of which could and should have been prevented had a more thoughtful approach to the problem been adopted. Even the ability to swim can often be more of a hindrance than a help for in cold, rough, wintry weather so much heavy clothing is needed to keep warm and dry that a strong swimmer would soon find himself in difficulties if pitched over the side without some form of lifesaving equipment. The drag of waterlogged gear and the numbing effect of icy-cold water are enough to beat the best of swimmers in a surprisingly short time. The danger is reduced if one has a companion aboard but even then teamwork and co-operation are essential in a small boat if disaster is to be averted. I well remember one Christmas on the Norfolk Broads some years ago, moored to the bank of a small cutting, fishing hard to obtain a supply of livebait for a day's piking. I stood up in the boat with my companion, Bob Ranby, operating from the bank. With a good supply of roach in the net I decided that one last cast would be enough but unbeknown to me Bob had quit fishing already and had started to climb aboard. After a bitter cold night there was a considerable amount of ice about and Bob lost his footing and fell lengthways along the gunwale, his sixteen-and-a-half stones being more than enough to capsize the seven-feet-seven-inch

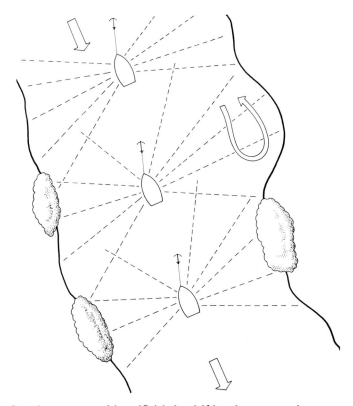

Covering a water with artificials by drifting downstream in stages.

Gremlin dinghy. I somersaulted neatly into the air executing as neat a jack-knife entry into the water as one could ever hope to see; Bob too, took to the water but fortunately we were both able to scramble out quickly and suffered no ill effects except the loss of a day's piking, which was plenty bad enough for me. The incident did however drive home most forcibly the lesson that teamwork is essential if two or more anglers are afloat at the same time in a small boat so some benefit at least was derived from the day's disaster.'

I have had my own share of dangerous moments in boats and it is only mildly reassuring to hear Ray state that being able to swim is hardly an advantage, because I do do not think I could, if encumbered with clothes and waders. On a couple of occasions I have had mild duckings from the bank and on one occasion actually stepped into twelve feet of water, in December, on my own. Because my waders filled with air

I came up feet first and had difficulty keeping my head above water. I floated downstream before catching hold of an overhanging willow and was then able to pull myself to the shore.

My old lifejacket has given up the ghost so I'll be looking around for a new one shortly. What I need is something I can comfortably get under my jacket. Let's face it, most lifejackets are cumbersome and get in the way of mobility and fishing – but obviously the matter cannot be treated lightly. When one is roughed up by a storm in the middle of a big Irish lough one needs *something*, because if the boat capsizes one would be unlikely to come out alive.

George Higgins and Barrie Rickards afloat on Lough Allen in Ireland (Eire). The fish weighed 14¾lb and was one of several good fish caught trolling on a two-day visit to the area by the author.

Many accidents in boats are caused by defects in the equipment provided, especially when a boat is hired. Why angling boats have rowlocks and loose oars is beyond my understanding. They should have thole pins and the oars should be attached so that they do not jump off, yet when not in use they may be stowed neatly along the gunwales, largely tucked out of the way. It's a help too if the boat doesn't leak: silly though that may sound I've had them often enough before the days of fibre glass. The anchors usually comprise the most serious defect, assuming some are provided. Almost always the rope is poor, too short and the anchor itself dubious. I suspect the only way is to have your own anchors. Mud anchors are fine for most waters but you need a range of weights, perhaps up to 20 lb or so. They can be made of concrete in a can, with a good ring set in a tangle of wire within the concrete. Ideally, the can should be removed because it can be nasty when it rusts. A plastic bucket is easier to remove.

Make sure you have a good hundred feet of rope. If you are to be anchored at both ends the whole lot needs duplicating. You can buy proper anchors with good tines and most have a useful breakaway system in that the rope goes through a 'weak' ring at the top of the shank and hence down to the gape or blades. Should you snag up seriously, in rocks, a really hard pull will open the ring and the anchor can be pulled out backwards. When anchored in a storm in deep water you can be in real danger if your anchor fouls and cannot be removed — it is not safe to ride out the storm. Far better is it to attach a float to the rope and cast it adrift. Any attempt to heave it free may submerge the bows unless it's a proper anchor. If you do a lot of piking from boats it really is advisable to go into a ships' chandlers to seek help, though it is important to explain exactly what you want to do.

Use of anchors is quite a difficult business in anything other than a gentle breeze. I think you need to be on as short a rope, or ropes, as possible but in a good blow you may need to pay out a good length — the bottom conditions, depth, and wind strength are all variables. And should you be part of a team do make sure that you are all trying to do the same thing. The first job is to try to work out where you want to be, and often it is a help to get upwind of that spot and come at it in stages, practising use of the anchors as you go. That's assuming you want two anchors out for bait fishing or for spinning from a fixed boat. Bows into the wind on a longish rope, with a shorter, steadying rope on the stern is another technique. In reasonable conditions you can manage with one rope on the bows, or one at each end dropped vertically.

For mobile fishing, say trolling or drift spinning, you need some combination of outboard engine, oars, drogue or otter/gunwale board — not necessarily all four at once! To my mind the use of an outboard on appropriate tick-over speed is a skilful business. I've done it often enough on my own, but my most recent experience was with George Higgins and colleagues from the Northern Irish Pike Society. I think I spent more time watching them operate, in three-foot-high waves, than I did actually concentrating on my fishing. Anyway, we caught a few fish even though snagging up on the bottom several times, which, when the wind blows, is a disconcerting experience. For drifting the drogue is easy enough to use, but a gunwale board takes more than a little practice. The gunwale board can, however, be set so that you can drift alongside a reed bed even though the wind seems to be blowing you into it! I could have done with such a device during my stay in Ireland, because I spent much of my time fighting to keep the craft out of the reed beds as I played, one-handed, a double figure pike.

Ardlui, the north end of Loch Lomond, from where many large pike have come. The author's boat and brolly can be seen on the small island from where, on the same morning, he took his best Lomond pike of 24½ lb.

I haven't touched the half of boating for pike as yet. If fishing baits on an anchored position it is quite possible to let the wind do plenty of work for you, either by creating a floating bow in your line or by using a drifter float. In addition you can use ordinary float fished, paternostered or ledgered baits. It pays not to try to do too much at the same time or the swing of the boat can create havoc and numerous false runs. When trolling, you can set the rods in outriggers and troll in the traditional manner, judging the depth fished by the weight of the lure, the length of line out, and a bit of trial and error. Or you can be thoroughly modern and use an echo sounder either with traditional trolling rigs or with downriggers on board. Downriggers help you control the depth very precisely, as do echo sounders of course.

However, when using an echo sounder alone the fact that you get little warning of a sudden depth change means that in practice your lure tends to run up and down the slope you are trying to follow. This in itself may be very appealing to the pike. In any event 'following a chosen contour' is almost a time-honoured way of catching good pike. Another good tip when trolling or drift spinning is to chuck a buoy over the side after you have taken a fish – mark the spot in other words, because there may be more down there.

I want to return now to what goes on in the boat itself. You cannot be too tidy. Moreover it is very necessary to clear a good space should you have to bring a pike on board. Most modern anglers have at least a sack on the floor, preferably foam rubber, to cushion the pike from damage. Having netted the fish, do not immediately haul it aboard – hang the net on the rowlocks or thole pin until you are quite ready for it with space, unhooking gear, weighing net, and cameras. Once you have the fish on board, hold it down with a wet cloth to stop it leaping about. Then proceed to unhooking in the normal way.

Gently returning a boat-caught pike on a small Irish loch.

CHAPTER EIGHT

Pike on the bank

The actual landing of pike and their handling on the bank is one area of enormous improvement during the last decade. The gaff, to which I always objected, not because it was 'cruel' but because it was inefficient, has all but disappeared. Those few people seen with gaffs are rightly laughed at as rank amateurs. The big, soft landing net is quite ideal. I only have one grouse about landing nets and that is that the triangular net is nothing like as efficient as a thirty-inch diameter round net. Yet triangular nets are the only ones readily available on the market. The tackle trade could certainly make improvements here and, at the same time, make quite a killing in terms of sales.

Another tool I am pleased to see the back of is the gag. Nowadays anglers use a glove and forceps. Gags, deep disgorgers, long-nosed pliers and the like have been shown to be entirely unnecessary, and I'm not now convinced that the gag is a useful tool to help train the newcomer to piking. The truth is that today the pike is less regarded as an object to fear. For hundreds of years fear alone has ruled the way in which

John Sidley with a fast water, weirpool pike of 17 lb. John specialises in river piking and is an expert at fishing fast waters.

96

anglers have treated pike; now that fear is going, season by season, so are the crude methods, the wanton killing, the tentative, over-cautious unhooking method, and so on.

Pike must be one of the few big predators that do not attack you. Just think what your chances would be of unhooking a shark, a crocodile or a dog – you'd be attacked! Pike are not aggressive in any way except when hungry, and they don't eat humans (or horses or swans or farmers' dogs). They eat fish. I do recall an incident that convinced one man otherwise! My wife had just landed a 22 lb pike on a fenland drain. It had been unhooked and lay quietly across the net whilst Laurie Manns got the camera ready. All morning we'd been pestered by another, very restless, piker who'd spent more time wandering up and down, talking to anyone daft enough to listen, than he had fishing. And he had this awful little rat of a dog that yapped incessantly. When he saw the fish being landed he came up to watch (and talk), and as the pike lay quietly he made the dreadful mistake of standing within a foot of its head. The pike then decided to do what they often do: it opened its mouth widely and shook its head from side to side. In the splittest of seconds the man's brand new, posh green waders were lacerated in several places as the big teeth shredded the rubber. Of course, we couldn't stand up for laughing and as my wife slid the fish back into the depths he became quite abusive to us. Matters were made worse by Laurie who, through his tears, said 'I shouldn't shake your leg mate or your toes might rattle about'. Fortunately he and his dog packed

Receiving advice from his dog, Paul Cullen plays in a big Irish pike. Caught without a landing net (the author had it in *his* boat!), Barrie Cooke, the Irish painter, prepares a hand gaff for the landing.

up and left the water. I thought about it afterwards and concluded that had he not had his big feet just where they were, the little dog would have been there, temporarily yapping. That *would* have been nasty.

However, you do get a little warning before a pike on the bank shakes his head as the body stiffens and flexes. Simply hold it down firmly with a hand at each end and you'll have no trouble.

The author lands a double-figure fish during a pike match. Note that the net is sunk and ready, and that the fish is on just the right length of line for netting. *Photograph: Ray Gregory.*

Playing pike

I don't intend saying much about playing pike. Normal big fish pumping methods are used. I usually like to get my fish on the bank quickly so that they are fresh enough to be returned speedily and in good health. The exception is when the fish is at depth on hooking, or when the weather is hot. I have a feeling, which may be quite wrong, that the risk of a gassed-up pike (fortunately a rare phenomenon anyway) is increased by hammering the fish under such circumstances. I am now a little more gentle; and, of course, warm water pike tend to fight harder and the quieter approach may lead to a quieter fight. I think.

Netting

Again I prefer to net the fish early, given an opportunity. To this end I maintain a low profile as the fish nears the net, crouching so low that the water often runs down the back of my waders! When you net a fresh fish it is lively in the net for a few seconds, but with today's small mesh, soft nets this hardly matters much. Once it has expended this bit of energy, this show of defiance perhaps, it can be quickly unhooked.

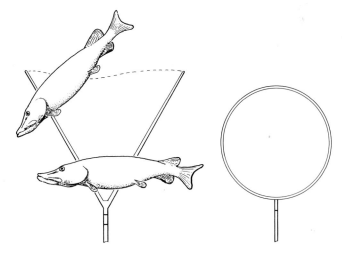

Triangular landing net frame with pike in awkward positions: effective netting area is considerably reduced, and is less than the overall 'smaller' round-framed net shown on the right.

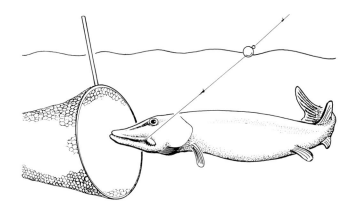

Allowing a big pike to swim into a deeply sunk net.

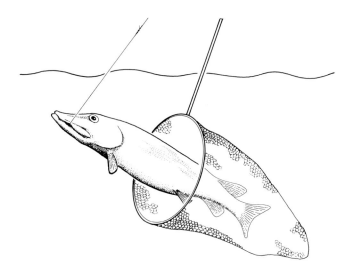

'Scooping' a pike lying awkwardly in the current. Note that modern micromesh netting makes this task more difficult as the current may really grip the netting causing severe problems especially if *a triangular net* is in use.

How to net a big fish: either take the strain on the frame (as shown), or lift the netting alone. The author here nets a fish for his wife, Christine, on Loch Lomond.

Unhooking

In 1984 I early decided to wear a glove on my left hand and have done so ever since, seeing little advantage in spending half the day bleeding from minor cuts. A soft, thick, leather gardening glove is ideal. They come in a bright yellowish colour as a rule. The index finger of the gloved left hand is inserted between the bony gill cover and the gill filaments, and the fish can be lifted off the ground. As the fish is lifted its mouth opens, or can be opened by pushing the upper jaw gently with the (gloved) thumb. Another advantage of the glove is that should the pike attempt to leap at this stage, the jaw line can be gripped firmly so that the fish does not fall. The soft leather clearly helps here because the teeth dig into it, but not into you; and the pike is secure but unharmed. The forceps are held in the right hand. All these instructions are simply reversed for the left-handed angler, naturally. If a friend is with you it always helps if he holds the trace for you, but should you be on your own, simply loop the trace around your (gloved) thumb if you wish to keep it taut. If you haven't left the run too long the fish should not be too deeply hooked and it is often quite unnecessary to have to hold the trace taut.

Basic method of unhooking pike of *any* size. It would be safer, with this big fish, to have a soft leather glove on the left hand because a tooth could go right through an unprotected hand.

Bait size

Let me digress at this stage to discuss the question of bait size. People get it into their heads from time to time that large baits are necessary for big pike. I do think there is some truth in this, but even so a great many big fish can be caught on baits in the 2 – 5 oz category. And the huge advantage of such bait sizes is that you never have to worry about whether the pike has them in its mouth; if it hasn't, it's a small one. So that once the run is going steadily, say a few yards at most, you can strike. Large baits introduce uncertainty and are best avoided.

Striking

There are two commonly adopted angles of striking: roughly parallel to the ground, and vertically upwards. On balance I prefer the second. Having tried both quite often I do not subscribe to the view that a low angle strike pulls the hooks into the corners of the pike's mouth; I have found no evidence of a direct relationship here. Nor do I believe that the vertical strike drives the hooks into the bony roof of the pike's mouth. What happens inside the pike's mouth depends upon a number of factors including the manner and firmness with which the bait is gripped, the way in which the line (trace) comes out of the mouth, *as well as* the angle of the strike itself. There is also some adjustment as the angler tightens up the line prior to the strike.

There are also two ways of actually sweeping home the strike: one is to tighten right up until you feel the fish, the other to 'guestimate' the amount of loose line remaining and to take it out on the strike. I use the second method, which gives the pike less chance to feel resistance and reject the bait. However illogical it may sound I'm sure this is the wrong method – but I cannot kick the habit! What I try to do sometimes is to wind up very gently until I feel the fish, but this cannot be done at long range.

On the other hand I cannot be doing much wrong, for as I write this in the 'summer' of 1985 I have only missed one run, and of all those fish landed not even one has had the hooks as far back in the mouth as the softer throat tissue. I describe elsewhere the hook rigs and hook types so I shall not repeat that here.

Weighing

Once again I have seen considerable improvements. This time in the weighing of fish. I am not, in fact, against hanging a fish on the hook of the balance because I really believe it does them no harm whatsoever. Even if they leap, which is unusual if you time things correctly, they'll only fall a short distance and then on to grass or foam (if you are doing the job properly). However, there are other ways of doing it. One is to use one of the excellent weighing bags which *should be dampened* before the pike is put in them. And do not forget to adjust the balance to zero with the net only on it, before weighing (or *deduct the weight of the net!*). Wet nets weigh a great deal more than people think and have contributed to not a few spurious claims.

Ray Webb taking a girth measurement of one of the fattest pike ever recorded—length: 34½″, weight: 20¾ lb. And this fish *was not* from a trout water.

Fish can be retained quite happily in keep sacks (or big weighing sacks which are little different) but if they are so retained they will be very lively indeed if you then take photographs of them later. So be prepared. In general it is better to take photographs quickly and then return the fish. It should not, however, be thought that putting fish in a keepsack or keepnet does them any harm because it does not.

The problem of so-called gassed-up pike is real, difficult, but fortunately rare. It's only happened to me once and the fish recovered when I pegged it out in a quiet spot with sticks and left it for an hour, quietly checking at intervals to see that it hadn't keeled over to one side. I do not believe it has been established with certainty that the fish *is* full of air, though some very experienced anglers do believe this. One successful way of helping such pike recover has been devised by Terry Eustace and friends: they sink the pike in deep water and leave it overnight (by deep I mean upwards of ten feet). Provided the bottom conditions are oxygenated, not foetid, the fish seem to recover quite well. Of course, this can only be done from a boat.

You can see, I think, that now we know what we are doing, handling of pike is really quite straightforward. Because they do not attack you it's simply a matter of controlling any leaping they may do, so that they do themselves no damage, and the kid glove technique protects both the fish and your hands. The only real problem, from the pike's point of view, is from handling by beginners – and that's where the Pike Anglers' Club comes in.

CHAPTER NINE

Surviving the elements

In order actually to record weather conditions it is a help to have some equipment – yet more things to carry. However, all that is needed is a thermometer, a light-meter and a barometer. I shall tackle the business of barometric pressure and piking later in this chapter, and suffice it to say about light-meters that I have never managed to sport one for photographic purposes, let alone fishing. Such factors as sun, cloud and wind have to be recorded with a good eye as far as I am concerned. We are left with the problem of a thermometer. Various angler's thermometers are available nowadays, yet they all seem a little expensive to me. For years I used a little tiny alcohol thermometer that goes by the brand name of 'Autotherm'. The cost at one of the chain stores, Woolworths I think, is not unreasonable, which, considering the rate at which I lose small items of tackle, is just as well for me. First of all I check my buy against a sophisticated laboratory thermometer, then I carefully wrap up any breakable edges in Elastoplast, and finally I drop it into an old foam-lined case. In such a condition it can be thrown thirty yards with no risk of breakage. I lose mine by leaving them in the water after taking the temperature or by treading on them when paddling in the shallows. Like trout fishermen, pike anglers also like to paddle.

I very much doubt whether any pike angler of the future will discover a temperature band in which all pike in all waters are on the feed. The whole point about noting water and air temperature is, as Ray says, to ascertain the pattern for *your* water. The same goes for other weather factors as well, except for barometric pressure, as I shall explain shortly.

There is *one* definite correlation between pike and water temperature, and that concerns fighting ability. On all waters of my experience the pike fight less well when the water temperature drops to around 40°F.

Ray Webb carefully returning a good twenty-pounder to the water. Note the thick winter clothing!

This happens long before pike become heavy with spawn, and it is a good water where the pike battle well after November. There are always exceptions, the occasional individual fish that would fight if frozen solid, but in general the rule holds. I usually find that anglers who claim that 'their' water holds the hardest-fighting pike in Britain have only fished for them in summer. Some of the colder, faster rivers, and some of the wilder lochs and loughs may be exceptions, in that pike quite used to cold water and pike that have never heard a human footfall, always tend to fight well. Even so, my own experience of Lomond is that what I have said holds true there also. As soon as it gets really cold the fighting ability, especially the ability and tendency to leap, declines quickly.

An example taken from the autumn of 1970 will suffice to illustrate the fall-off in fighting ability. Between October 1st and the beginning of November I had a considerable number of hard fighting double-figure pike, to all methods, and including a number of 20-pounders. The last two twenties in this spell were taken on successive casts and weighed 20½ and 26 lb respectively. Both fell to half-mackerel ledgered at sixty yards' range, and both gave tremendous battles, the smaller fish giving me the greatest battle I have ever had with any fish. On a typical run the fish would take ten to fifteen yards of line, pause for a split second, and, before I could even think of pumping it back, take another ten or fifteen yards. At one point in the fight I had eighty yards of line off the spool, and was beginning to think about losing my first 30-pounder . . . It took a full fifteen minutes before it charged at full speed into a half-sunken landing net.

Still trembling and aching I unhooked the half-mackerel from its lower jaw, and looked up just in time to see a column of spray about sixty yards away as a hunting pike lashed at the surface over fifteen feet of water. I quickly popped the 20-pounder into a keepnet, and, using the same tackle and half-mackerel, punched the bait out to the feeding fish. About five minutes later, during which time I had recovered somewhat, I saw the line streaming off the spool and the float nowhere in sight. Another hefty strike, this time into a fish almost eighty yards distant, and another powerful fight lasting about seven or eight minutes and the 26-pounder finally hit the net. Ray had done the 'double' several years ago, and it was really great to tell him about this catch.

Three weeks later the water temperature was down around 40°F and the pike came in like lambs, relatively speaking anyway. The same thing happens every year on most of the waters I fish, but I am not certain whether the 'rule' applies to waters like Lough Ree, which never really get cold.

A final comment on really low temperatures is prompted by Ray's remarks about Hornsea Mere and the bitter easterly winds which so often seem to sweep it. I remember spending two long days there one winter, two days without a run, and with a searing and constant easterly blast. At around 4 p.m. on the second day, just when I got a faint feeling that we might get a run on herring, one of the boat's occupants who was huddled on the bottom boards like the rest of us, started sobbing. We should have realised much earlier, when he went quiet in fact, that he was suffering from exposure. This is the nearest we have ever come to losing someone through exposure to the elements, and it certainly isn't a matter to be taken lightly even in England. Under such extreme weather conditions the right sort of clothes are important; a modicum of common sense is better still.

Pike and light conditions make an interesting study. Ray Webb has a thing about thick fog, and my experiences are similar to his. Fog in the fens fills one with confidence. It is also true that many waters go well at dawn and dusk when the light is weakest, most pike anglers arriving two hours after dawn and leaving one hour before dark. Some of our leading anglers have made the same observations about roach, and, indeed, it may be the feeding activities of this and other food fishes which helps to set the pike feeding. There are certainly risks of circular arguments here, and yet both pike and big roach may come on the feed because they need the cover of semi-darkness.

We have a very impressive case of light affecting the feeding pike on December 26th, 1970. Several of the Cambridgeshire Pike Anglers were fishing a fenland drain under quite bright, even sunny conditions. By 11.30 a.m. we had very little to show for 3½ hours of effort when a snow storm blotted out the rosy scene for about fifteen minutes. During that time we had six runs on ledgered herrings and mackerel resulting in fish of 13½ lb; 18½ lb; 14¼ lb; and 10½ lb, plus two dropped baits.

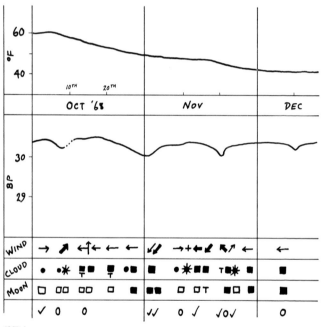

KEY:

✓ Big Pike   O Bad Days
Wind: → Moderate W, ↘ Strong N.W, + No Wind
Cloud: ✳ Sun, ● Cloudy Bright, ■ Dull, T Rain
Moon: ☐ No Moon - clear, ■ Cloudy

The bare facts of 2½ months pike trips plotted graphically and pictorially, thus releasing the normal diary for ideas, feelings, conclusions etc.

One of the runs actually stopped as the sun came out again. We had no more runs for a long period, until the bright sun faded, in fact. Then followed fish of 14 lb; 14¾ lb; 9½ lb and 11¼ lb. Pike anglers who dismiss this sort of thing as coincidence will miss a lot of pike.

Night feeding pike

Night fishing for pike is here to stay and can reasonably be considered under the title of light conditions! Whether we will ever be able to predict *when* to night fish, I don't know. After all, it takes us all our time to predict when to day fish. Perhaps on some heavily fished waters *any* night fishing may yield results at first. I'm thinking here of a water such as Landbeach near Cambridge. Nowadays it yields few big pike but plenty of fish from 1 – 3 lb weight, and it is heavily flogged for these. One day during the 1966 winter I watched ten baits at work in one small deepish bay, the total result for a full day being a few fish up to 4 lb. After dark, when the rest of the anglers had packed up, I stayed on for several hours. I should point out that I was after pike-perch at the time and used scaled down pike gear, including tiny livebaits under 1 in. diameter floats, at a depth of about three feet. I had two or three small pike in the first two hours after dark, followed by a fish of 11 lb after three hours' fishing, a veritable monster of the water at this time. On subsequent trips we got our pike-perch and numbers of pike. It became clear that on this water the fish fed as freely after dark as during daylight hours. Conditions on each occasion were overcast, the only blank being on a bright moonlit night. The only other winter night blanks I have had have been under similar conditions, perhaps because there is usually a considerable drop in temperature, particularly if the day has been sunny. This fishing has been done only during the first few hours of darkness, since at that time I was neither mentally nor physically equipped to cope with a full, long winter-night session. I intend to do a lot more however. Summer night-fishing will, I suspect, turn out to be less spectacularly successful, if only because the pike have plenty of time to feed during the day. Small pike certainly feed well on some summer nights as every tench angler knows too well.

In my very early days of pike fishing I was quite unable to get results under really windy conditions, and to tell you the truth I preferred flat calm water surfaces where my large bung could be seen for miles. I now know that some of the waters I fished *do* fish well in those glassy calms, particularly on early summer mornings before the sun is up. I also know that my skill at tackle control was unable to face fishing in a strong north-westerly gale. Nowadays I prefer a stiff breeze, particularly if it does not impede tackle control or casting too much, and it is quite surprising how often the wind can be made to work for you. Wind is a great asset if the pike angler wants to drift a suspended deadbait, or make a float-ledgered deadbait drag slowly round in a wide arc.

I used to have a nasty little ruse to get round choppy conditions on some small pike waters; as I say, *any* wind was detrimental when I first started. This consisted of tying some cord around a half-pound block of margarine, setting it to the depth of the water, putting a stone on the other end and then heaving it out into some unobtrusive spot in the lake where it remained anchored to the bottom. Within a short time the choppy lake surface was reduced to a glossy if somewhat oily calm. I rather think that this technique might be frowned upon today, and would not encourage it as part of your repertoire. I discovered it, incidentally, when mashing up sandwiches into groundbait which was then heaved around the pike bungs.

Smooth conditions are not necessarily detrimental to success as so many pundits seem to think. Indeed, if the light is poor, I am usually quite confident, other things being equal. Suspended deadbaits work well on glassy calm still waters, contrary to the popular idea that foot-high waves are required to give a suspended deadbait 'life'. Even under rough conditions the pike is quite fully aware that a suspended deadbait is stone dead, as evidenced by the fact that they will often prefer suspended deadbaits to suspended livebaits under both rough and calm conditions. Equally often they prefer the livebaits. The rough water has nothing whatever to do with the success of the dead as opposed to the livebait, of that I am certain.

From what has been written above it must be clear to the reader that in the writer's opinion nothing in the way of weather characteristics will form a key as to whether pike will be on the feed over a wide area. The great advantage of weather study in relation to pike is that it helps *you* to work out the pattern for *your* waters. Never believe that definite recognisable patterns do not exist.

Having said that I shall return, with some unease, to the subject of barometric pressure and big pike. First of all there are several problems to think about, to which I can provide no answers. One is that pike should not know anything about atmospheric pressure changes. After all, water was incompressible when I was a schoolboy, and I understand it still is. Again, most pike traverse considerable depths; they will often come up from the bottom in twenty feet of water and take a livebait fished two feet deep. When they do this the water pressure upon their bodies must change dramatically. Why should they worry about relatively minute atmospheric pressure changes? I can offer no answers, except to suggest that pike, and other fish, living in the dense medium of water, may be acutely perceptive of what appear to us as tiny changes in conditions.

I will say categorically that there *is* a relationship, probably a direct relationship, between the feeding of big pike and the pressure patterns. This being the case one would expect pressure to have a wide geographical effect on feeding since a trough may embrace the whole of Britain at once, whereas sunshine, wind, cloud cover, fog, frost and all the other variables are essentially local features even within a single pressure system. I think this is actually the case, for how often do we read in the angling press of a 'pike week', or a 'bream week' for that matter, when all the pike in the country seem to be on the feed? Editors and newspaper-men have assured me that they do not hold back information in order to make a 'pike week', so *something* brought the pike in general on the feed. I would contend that it is *not* temperature, or rain, or cloud cover etc. since these are so variable from area to area. In fact, the pike have responded to widespread, controlling barometric pressure regimes.

It seems to me that when there is a sudden, big, sustained pressure rise after, say, two or three weeks when the barometer has been either very low or very variable, then the pike come on the feed with a vengeance. A sustained very low pressure regime, sustained for a week or more, often sends the fenland pike quite 'off' moving baits such as livebaits and spinners, and yet many feed exceptionally well on ledgered herrings and mackerels. I am a practical angler, not a theorist, and it is fortunate that these ideas are based not so much upon watching press reports for several years, but upon the capture by myself and eight friends of over 500 pike in excess of 10 lb in three years. I *know*, on our waters, that excessive, sustained, low pressures will result in the pike feeding well on ledgered herrings. Big pressure rises tend to make them forget herrings and hunt more actively for livebaits. The Christmas weekend of 1970, for example, was accompanied by a marked, but not sustained low-pressure regime, and several of us on a fen drain had nearly twenty runs on ledgered mackerel resulting in about fifteen pike over 10 lb, and one of 20½ lb to Mick Griffiths. Less than half this number of runs were obtained on livebaits and these were mostly small fish around 4–8 lb. Had the low pressure been more sustained it would have been unusual to get any runs on livebaits.

Others have noted a marked correlation between pressure and eel feeding spells, without as yet having carried out statistical tests. Terry Coulson also considers that the graphs I have kept for several years are strongly suggestive of a relationship between pressure and pike (and other species). Some anglers with whom I have discussed these problems have suggested that the relationship might not be *direct*, but might involve a linked system such as phytoplankton to food fish to pike. Clearly, ideas of this kind will take some testing but for our purpose the link of barometric pressure to pike will do as a working relationship. The diagram gives some actual examples of results versus pressure graphs. I would just add that *extreme* local conditions such as torrential rain, floods, or snow water may affect the piking more strongly than what I now regard as the overall controlling factor, namely barometric pressure. That the picture may be yet more complicated than the way I have painted it, is suggested by the fact that on some of our local drains even a rapidly rising barometer may bring the fish on the feed on one section of the system only! It may be, of course, that that was the only section with fish in it (see Chapter Eleven)!

Standard barometers, normally adorning hallways or doctors' surgeries, can be studied before going fishing and after returning. However, I have a small pocket model, like a folding alarm clock. This I find is a great deal more convenient than going to the doctor, for Christine refuses to have a barometer hanging in the hall.

Work in North America should cause us to think a little bit harder about the elements. Normally, with respect to (Northern) pike, we in these islands are streets ahead of the U.S.A., but on some matters they are ahead of us, as on the subject of lure fishing, for example. Weather study may be another plus factor for trans-Atlantic pikers even though they have not yet tagged on to barometric pressure as *the* factor. I refer to the work reported in *In-Fisherman* magazine on oxygen content of the water and on pH readings.

I have to dismiss pH readings at the moment because I have no experience of recording pH variations against fishing results day by day. Nor do I understand the logic behind the thinking, for pH values on the waters of my experience seem to vary little, even from season to season. But I keep an open mind as *In-Fisherman* has pioneered many things in angling on that continent.

Neville Fickling with a Norfolk Broads fish of 41 lb 6 oz which held the record at this weight for a short while, and subsequently at a higher weight when it was caught again by Derrick Amies. Neville has been one of the pioneers of returning to the water alive and well what used to be called 'trophy' pike.

Oxygen content *must* be important. There may be a relationship here with barometric pressure in that low pressures mean lower oxygen content (in effect, the air pressure pushes fewer oxygen molecules into the surface layers of the water, yet allows dissolved oxygen to escape more easily from the surface film). High pressure means exactly the opposite. It is of interest that under high pressure regimes I would maintain that pike feed more actively, taking not only deadbaits, but also livebaits and spinners; indeed they may completely ignore static baits. This is exactly the same as human beings, not that we would take livebaits and spinners, but we *are* more active when the pressure is high, and we feel relatively sluggish when it is low (we are able to breathe less oxygen into our lungs simply because the air pressure is less and contains fewer oxygen molecules per given volume – each breath gets less).

Oxygen content in the water is not only controlled by barometric pressure but by a whole host of other factors such as a supply of oxygen-rich water from a side stream, the amount of decaying organic matter (e.g. algae) in suspension and so on. There is, therefore, a case for using an oxygen meter – one *more* thing to carry. There is no doubt in my mind that in today's electronic world there will soon be a single piece of wizardry which will record oxygen, barometric pressure, temperature, pH and probably other things as well. I look forward to the day, because I should like to know not only where the various temperature layers are in which I fish, but also their oxygen content. Something, or a combination of things, does put pike at particular depths in a water and I'm quite sure we often totally miss them in our efforts to put a bait on the bottom. The modern graph recorders (such as the Lowrance fish finders) do show that whereas pike in our waters often *are* deep, they are not always so, but may be 'stratified'.

Thus I am sure that barometric pressure rules when it comes to how and on what pike will feed, but that does not tell us *where* they will feed. Whilst we are thinking about the U.S.A., what about their 'moon-phase charts'? We have always laughed at them, but why? Sea anglers know that tides are quite vital to their fishing, and that tides are largely governed by the moon. However gentle the effects must be, all freshwaters must also be affected by tidal influence. Presumably we do not have the instruments to detect the changes as 'tides', but we *can* check the phases of the moon. The kind of recording chart I depict can be used for recording anything, of course, and in doing it in this way the various elements of the weather can be checked one against the other. I am sure some enterprising young piker could computerise the whole thing and possibly decipher relationships, testing them for validity.

Clothes for the pike angler

So far I have been discussing the weather from one point of view only, namely that of the pike. But *we* have to survive the weather too! In the early 1970s we were ill-equipped to combat the bitter winter, and I simply opted for a Barbour jacket overlapping my waders and varied the numbers of old sweaters underneath. I virtually lived in them – and I lined my waders with fur! Today we have a variety of jackets and suits available, and one of them, the one-piece Bob Church suit, is certainly worthy of special mention. But we also have thermal underwear and socks – all expensive but quite indispensable, especially as you get older. Insulated boots too – how on earth did we manage without them? The moon boot waders, whilst having some drawbacks (such as the tops coming off!) are excellent for winter fishing and I am sure that eventually they will replace conventional waders. So a long discourse is unnecessary now on what to wear. Get good underwear and good overwear, water- and wind-proof. In thirty years I have got through three Barbour jackets. Two I still have, and one I still use even though my friends consider it down at heel! Recently I reproofed it – at least I did the cloth around the holes! When I went up to collect my draw ticket in the A.C.A./Angling Times National Pike Angling Championships a raucous voice from the back of the crowd shouted 'Why doncher git a noo jackit?' I'll continue to wear it, because it's an old favourite, but before long I shall have to move into the 1980s I suppose.

CHAPTER TEN

Pike location

There are basically two ways of finding pike. One is to follow the press reports, the other to find your own. I'll say a little about the first, but the second gives me greater satisfaction. And it does mean that if you are capable of working out for yourself where pike are, then you should be able to sort out that totally new water unaided by friends or press reports.

The main problem with following press reports, whether local or national, is that others are doing the same and the fishing may well be crowded. The same is true of finding waters via the notorious grapevine; that choice piece of secret information is, as often as not, shared by dozens of other anglers. You can, of course, learn a lot about pike just by being where they are, by catching them, even if you did little towards it yourself other than chuck out a bait or two. But I don't think you learn anything like as much. As a matter of fact I don't mind crowds as long as the individuals behave themselves. The trouble is that every crowd of anglers has a few idiots who in various ways spoil it for everyone else. With the best collective will in the world a crowd cannot help overfishing a water, and heavily fished waters do not usually last more than a couple of seasons. A good friend of mine and very fine piker, John Sidley, recently quoted me as saying that once you've had some good catches you should move on and let someone else have a share. In fact he misunderstood me, but what I do say is that once some piking I have discovered becomes crowded then I move on to pastures new. If no-one crowds me out I'm quite happy to go on catching good pike for ever!

There is, therefore, a number of short cuts you can take: the local angling column; the national newspapers and angling monthlies; the grapevine; the tackle shop, and so on. The information is variously second-hand and inaccurate, but eventually you'll find yourself on a water with big pike and big crowds. If you are successful you will have trouble, make no mistake whatever about that, as jealousy begins to rule. You will find that you have to get there earlier and earlier to find 'your' swim and groups of anglers may well sit on in rotation for weeks on end. In one instance I recall some anglers camping out for two days before the pike season opened so that they could beat me to a swim I had fished for several years before being discovered! They didn't just camp (which was breaking the rules) but they also fished out of season for pike. When I arrived at my customary hour before dawn I found not only the encampment, which astonished me enough, but was further astonished to discover that despite all their efforts and planning they had actually missed *the* hotspot (see next chapter) by a few yards. So I dropped in that spot myself and caught a fish of 20 lb. I thought that was reasonable justice, especially as they hadn't done that well. But I certainly went less often after that. Fish are not that important to me.

On another occasion a friend found that his favourite early season venue had been deliberately booked as a match length by some specimen hunters intent on getting the swims to themselves on opening day. My friend was actually moved out of the stretch by the Water Authority bailiff, whose hands were metaphorically tied, but he went on to catch double-figure pike when the 'match-men' failed! If you enjoy such competition then by all means hang on a crowded bandwagon.

Malcolm Bannister with a twenty-four-pounder from the Great Ouse.

Two further incidents spring to mind which I shall recount briefly. The first concerned three anglers who knew Ray and I were fishing the Lower Ouse, so they walked mile after mile until they found us! The second occurred when I was driving Laurie Manns out of Milton very early one morning. I turned on to the A10 from the village and saw in my mirror a car creep out of a side turning, on side lights. A short while further up the road, by varying our pace and watching the response I realised we were being followed. At Stretham we swapped drivers, I being a bit of a beginner and Laurie under training as a police driver at the time. We lost them in the back streets of Ely after Laurie gave an exhibition of cornering the likes of which I do not wish to experience again. But those two incidents are almost sporting and one doesn't mind too much.

Assuming from now on that you'll be trying to sort out your own waters, there still remain two basic problems: 1. is to find the water; 2. is to find the fish on it. If the water hasn't already been overfished then the pike might be quite localised, into hotspots, and these sometimes take some finding. Tackling hotspots is very important and I want to treat the whole subject more fully in the next chapter, so in this one I'll deal with every other aspect of pike location and lead up to the hotspot idea towards the end.

Finding a water with pike in it is not difficult as most have them. However, because of man's interference (see Chapter Twelve for details) quality piking is less common. Usually, waters that are heavily club-fished tend to have poor piking. Not always, of course, especially if the very presence of pike is unsuspected. Small waters, say under eight acres, are particularly at risk, the more so if they are shallow and weedy. Such waters may well hold fish over 20 lb, but not many, and if they have been badly handled by the inexperienced then they will not last long and the fishery declines into one full of tiny pike. Nevertheless, small lakes, even those heavily weeded in summer, can yield good pike to the careful angler. Park lakes are well worth attention. These often lack weed even when shallow because the amount of human debris thrown in is considerable. But sitting out in the middle of many a park lake is a good 20-pounder or two. One word of warning: should you catch one keep quiet about it, not just because such a lake can be quickly fished out, but because the local non-anglers suddenly discover that 'ducklings are being eaten' and 'horses have been pulled in' and 'children are at risk' and any number of other ludicrous and ill-founded fairy stories. *Don't* publish your capture in the local newspaper.

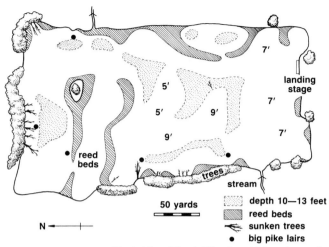

Newport Long Pond, East Yorkshire (North Humberside) as it was in the 1960s when 'discovered' by the author. In 1986 a 29 lb fish was caught, making the author's results look a bit puny!

Bigger lakes, clay pits and gravel pits, are a better bet for more consistent sport. I try to find waters which, ideally, are reputed to have no pike. Ideally they'll have no pike anglers either, and only once did I fish a water that genuinely had no pike. (It has now, though not, I hasten to add, as a result of anything I did.) Failing such ideal circumstances, choose one that isn't being pike fished, or was a decade or so ago but isn't now. You can also search your own region by means of an Ordnance Survey (1 : 50 000) map. Anything that shows up as a water on such a scale is worth investigating. Rivers and drains are also clearly indicated. Shallow, riffly rivers usually produce only the occasional big pike, so look for waters over six feet deep. Drains are a different matter entirely. I know drains in the fens which are two feet deep and about twelve feet wide, but they have numerous double-figure fish in them. In fact I do not know a drain in fenland which doesn't have pike over 20 lb. In other regions tiny drains may be less productive, as in the northwest. (It would be of interest to know why.)

As your interest and involvement grow you may wish to move out of your immediate neighbourhood, and then one has of necessity to take some notice of press reports, magazine articles and books. Even so, everyone knows that the Broads have been good for pike so your searching and investigating can be continued with a map once the basic decision to explore has been made.

By various means you arrive at a decision to give a water a try. What next? It is absolutely vital to use all the means at your disposal to make a detailed plan. This may involve aerial photographs, admiralty charts, town council plans, but mostly your own sketch plan. On this plan you need to mark 'North' so that you can judge the effect of wind whilst sitting at home. You also need the depth variations, nature of the bottom, positions and nature of weed beds, snags, and so on – a complete three-dimensional picture of the water. Use any and all means to find accurate depths – echo sounder; boat; float and plummet; Depth-o-plug; count-down method – and then relate the figures to an immovable object such as a mark on a bridge support. When you have a complete model of the water it is amazing what confidence it gives you. You know exactly where and why you are fishing all the time, so that a negative result becomes as important as a capture in building up the picture. You will, of course, be simultaneously recording the weather and feeding times.

That's the general scenario, so what about detailed clues? You can climb trees to spot pike or watch for them rolling or striking soon after dawn. Pike spend quite a lot of time near the surface, more than is commonly supposed, so just to sit quietly at dawn can be revealing. Some echo sounders will show up individual fish, of course, so there's a real short cut for you if you can use a boat on the water. You can also watch a water during the close season to see if they spawn in particular places. That gives you some idea of the size of pike in the water and also the rough position of March swims as the pike gather before spawning. Another method of finding pike is to throw out deadbaits, either in positions you can observe (as from a tree or boat) or attached to cotton. If they are taken it may be that you have found a feeding area. Of course, pike are attracted strongly by scent so you may have *created* a feeding area rather than finding a natural feeding ground. As you become more experienced it *is* possible to persuade pike to feed where you want them – as long as you feed them well enough and often enough. (This, like sophisticated echo sounders, is expensive and raises moral issues in the minds of some anglers, myself included.)

'Features' are always claimed by piking writers as holding areas and in this there is some truth, beyond doubt. I expand the question further in Chapter Eleven, but for the moment state that the following places *often* hold a pike or two (if not always very many): brick or concrete work of any kind (valve towers, bridges, dams); overhanging trees; submerged snags on a *clean* bottom; changes in slope; junction pools on rivers or drains; reedy margins with the reeds in deepish water; weed beds; rafts of weed or other debris; deep holes in relatively shallow water; inflowing fast water to a sluggish stream. Searching such places will yield pike, boost your confidence, and provide you with the occasional good fish or good catch. What it will not do is tell you where the *best* swims are on the water, not necessarily anyway.

Two other location methods need discussing: fry or prey shoals; and spinning. Spinning is one of the best and most enjoyable ways of locating pike, especially in the kind of holding hole I listed in the last paragraph. It may not produce many fish, but if a double-figure fish is caught, that particular place is worth a bit of attention for a while. Because small fish *are* prey, in any water, it follows that the pike must feed on them! So if you can locate the shoals of cyprinidae or perch then you must find some pike sooner or later. There are times when fry shoals always seem to have pike in attendance, as when fry are holed up in a bay by a number of pike which feed at intervals. Once again, however, this does not always mean that you will catch many fish, and fry shoals may move.

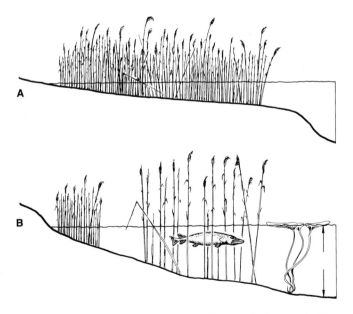

A; dense reed beds in shallow water: not usually a good pike margin. B; margin with sparse reeds in which pike can get good cover.

You can do everything I have described in the last few paragraphs, catch nice fish, have good sport, and yet still completely miss what the water really has to offer in the way of big pike and big catches. This is because pike tend to be holed up in hotspots, like lions at their lair, and whilst they'll feed well if you drop a bait on their noses, you'll only otherwise catch them when they are out hunting. I do not believe that pike are basically solitary as textbooks often claim. Holding spots will, as I explained above, hold a few fish because they are good ambush points, especially for smaller pike which may well need the additional aid of an ambush point as an element of surprise. Other spots may be what I have often called transient hotspots, such as several good pike in attendance on a fry shoal which may never again stop in that place. So, I have gone round and round the mulberry bush, but have eventually led you to the concept of hotspots, so do read on.

I think I ought to postscript this chapter by saying that I still believe you cannot guarantee to find 30-pounders (as distinct from big doubles and 20-pounders) by my preferred methods. You need the short cut, news reports-cum-grapevine method, so I'll leave it to you to decide whether a 30-pounder is that important. I've still managed to get two!

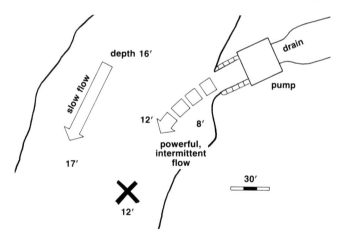

A pike hotspot on a Fenland river.

CHAPTER ELEVEN

Pike lairs

In the previous chapter I described a kind of pike lair, the holding hole which temporarily holds an individual pike or small group of pike. What I want to talk about now are real hotspots. I shall talk of them as fact, because I believe they exist. To be fair, some experienced anglers, perhaps rather few of them, do not believe in hotspots, preferring to use the principles of the last chapter to find all their pike and explain all their captures this way. They attribute great mobility to the pike, which I would not deny. But the mobility of a pike after capture is no real guide to how it *normally* behaves. Even so, it is surprising how often returned pike will swim back to what I term a hotspot, despite being put back more than a mile away in some cases. And hunting pike do travel and patrol in ways that will get them a few meals. Like all predators they are skilful at tracking their quarry and they'll move a long way. Quite often, however, and possibly for most of their lives *big* pike are holed up quietly together, often in quite large numbers. Find them, catch them as they come to feed, and you'll get those 200 lb bags or a dozen double-figure fish at a sitting.

So what is a hotspot? It is a small area, sometimes of the order of thirty yards by ten yards, in which large numbers of big pike are holed up for much of the time except when out on a hunting spree (as during a big high pressure period). A hotspot is identified as readily by the failure of rods only a few yards away as by the catches within it. One hotspot on the Relief Channel was on only ten yards of the bank and seemed to be largely in the middle of the water (again roughly ten yards by thirty yards). That spot fished well for several years before being discovered by others. In that time it yielded a great many big double-figure pike, including nearly thirty 20-pounders. Outside the spot, *despite more rods being fished*, only three 20-pounders were taken and far, far, fewer doubles.

I could list you dozens of examples. One I have been fishing now for eight years and have had almost all my 20-pounders on that water from an area only ten yards long, and 60 per cent of my doubles as well. Provided the pike are handled well, such hotspots last a long time. The feeding in them seems to be of two kinds: either they feed a little, for a short time, most days; or they go out on a hunting spree. The second, which is less frequent than you might think, accounts for those occasions when every pike on the water seems to be on the feed and they are caught far and wide. If you can catch such a feeding spell at its beginning you may well hold them in the hotspot just by the smell of your bait and the free offerings you give them, and a big catch can result.

The author's concept of a hotspot on a small Fenland drain: half the width of the drain is shown, and a depth of about three feet. Such a swim may be twenty yards long, and number *one* for every *two miles* of water.

It ought to be said that I have had offered to me an alternative explanation of hotspots, namely, that the pike do not actually live there but *feed* there on their way through or on visitations. Against this is the almost damning evidence that rods fished either side fail completely most of the time. If they ignore *all* baits until they get to the hotspots it supposes a quite astonishing timing on their part, or a special attraction of the hotspot itself. This raises the next feature of hotspots or, rather, lack of feature. Very, very rarely are you able to relate a hotspot to a physical feature or the presence of a roach shoal. I believe myself that shoals of cyprinidae which pass along the water get chomped if they choose the wrong time to go through. Pike often come on the feed so suddenly – adjacent rods getting runs simultaneously – that the prey fish are probably caught unawares and may, indeed, themselves act as a trigger if they pass by at a bad time (for them, that is!).

A few years ago the members of the Cambridgeshire Pike Anglers, nine of them, identified a hotspot some twenty to thirty yards long on a fenland drain. By really squeezing things three or four anglers could fish the hotspot and the rest fished along either side of them upstream and down. Usually only two were in the hotspot, in fact, so that when we consider total catches for one season, listing them as 'hotspot' versus 'the rest', it was 'the rest' that actually received most attention – the greater number of rod-days if you prefer to put it that way. Of eighteen 20-pound plus fish we took that year from the drain, fourteen came from the hotspot. Of the double-figure fish only 15 per cent were caught *outside* the swim, and we had a lot of double-figure fish. The sport was tremendous, and I cannot understand these people who claim to get fed up of catching big, hard-fighting pike. Naturally, we took turns in the swim, except when Laurie Manns, Christine and I were on the water when we crowded in together. We can fish half a dozen rods on a sixpence and only get them tangled up when Christine casts a spell on us. It is obvious from the above that the recognition of a hotspot is more easily achieved with a number of anglers. Several times on this water the pike came on the feed 'all over', or in other words they moved out of the hotspot on the rampage, but mostly, whilst big pike were taken regularly in the spot itself few were taken even thirty yards away.

Another way to find hotspots, less efficient than the teamwork mentioned above but useful for two anglers, is to 'leap frog' along the bank. Bill Chillingworth and I were doing this one winter on a stretch of drain we did not know well when eventually the leading rod found the fish. We moved into the area, and beyond it, but the fish were coming from a relatively short stretch of some twenty to thirty yards. It turned out to be a transient hotspot – a short-lived one, but more interesting to us was the fact that one particular place in the swim consistently yielded double-figure fish one after another. This area was about five feet out from the bank in quite shallow water, and if the bait was dropped in an area of some four feet by six then runs could be assured. The best fish weighed 19 lb. Outside this tiny area we had to wait much longer. Both of us have met the same thing in other hotspots. Even so, as long as the angler was in the hotspot area of some twenty to thirty yards of bank he was in with a good chance of consistent sport.

I have already implied that hotspots are very small compared to the size of the water. Hornsea Mere is 1½ miles long, but at the time we fished it there was only one hotspot discovered on the water in spite of heavy fishing. Similarly on Lough Ree, some 19 miles long, the local pike expert assured me that as far as he was concerned there were only about six really tremendous stretches on the lake. Although good fish were picked up everywhere from time to time (hunting pike) he regarded most of the lake as so much barren water. It took him ten to fifteen years to reach his conclusions, and life is too short to argue with him. He put me on to two of his hotspots and I began to take good fish. One of these swims had yielded him and his son some huge catches of pike to wagtails and large spoons, the best being a catch of five 20-pounders in one day as well as other good fish. This spot was approximately thirty yards by fifty, and boats away from the vicinity took hardly a fish. Before the other locals found out about it he had taken good catches for almost five years, and even during pike matches he was able to use a powerful outboard to reach the swim well before the others, take a fish or two, and then move away in order to keep it secret.

Most hotspots last from year to year and if fished by careful anglers can yield good sport indefinitely. Hornsea Mere was hammered unlike any water I have ever seen, and it lasted just three years, which is more a tribute to the resilience of its hard-fighting pike than to the common sense of the anglers who fished it. Ray and I were to a large degree responsible for letting the cat out of the bag, a thing we regret to this day. We will never knowingly do it again, for the ruination of a hotspot and often of the whole pike water, is a sad event. Hotspots are the reason for being very, very cagey about where you catch your fish; most of those I fish now would not last three years.

Well, why do pike choose to shoal up in such a small area on a big water? This is the question to which I have no reasonable answer. I know one or two hotspots that are in the region of some feature like a feeder stream or a sharp bend in the river. These places, as it happens, harbour shoals of roach and bream. Some of the hotspots on the drains I fish are in the region of huge bream shoals without actually being in the middle of the bream, and since it is common to find hotspots on one bank only, it is almost as if they leave a gap for the food fish to swim through when they are rash enough. But equally often there are no signs of roach and bream anywhere near the hotspot, which lends support to the idea that the hunting pike move out of the spot itself when really on the feed. The angler fishing a hotspot regularly will be fishing most of the time when the big pike are not really feeding. It is here, in the pike's lair as it were, that real finesse in piking technique counts. Methods which will easily take hunting pike – trolling, spinning, shallow livebaiting with a large bung and so on – may fail completely when free-line livebait, ledgered livebait and carefully presented stationary deadbaits may score heavily. The shallower the water, the truer the above statement seems to be.

But when the pike decide to feed in earnest the knowledgeable angler will be at the very focus, the starting point, of their feeding spree. Normally they will have a short feeding snack each day and in this case the angler will still be consistently successful (see Chapter Two on Feeding Patterns).

Now for that tight packing that I mentioned. I have spent some time on a tiny drain which is a mere twenty-one feet wide and several miles long. One of the hotspots is some sixty yards long – unusually long in fact – but within this stretch is a length of ten yards of bank which has yielded a large number of big double-figure pike to ledgered herrings, livebaits and artificials. The water is about three to four feet deep: you could work out the cubic footage as 4 ft x 30 ft x 21 ft. When it is considered that a big pike is between three and four feet long, you could get ten fish nose to tail in one line, and about the same number in a line side by side across the drain. One hundred big pike in such a small area might be exaggerating a fair bit, but nevertheless the less quantitative expression 'packed like sardines' conjures up the right sort of picture. I well remember Ernest Merrit's description of a vast hotspot shoal that he once found on Hornsea Mere, and it bore a close resemblance to the deductions above – and he caught 49 of them.

Obviously the bream shoals cannot often swim the gauntlet past pike concentrations of this nature – it would be suicidal. The pike must go on the hunt. But why then do they stay in one tiny area from season to season? Is it just possible that they ignore bream shoals swimming by until the concentration of them really is more than the pike can stand? As I said at the beginning, I have as yet no real reasons for hotspots in most cases, but they exist with a vengeance. Hot swims also survive temporary natural upsets such as floods. When a period of heavy rainfall sets in and water levels rise on a river, poor returns can be expected for a while. Once the dirt and debris clear away, a pike or two will usually turn up even if the water remains high. If the flood level persists for any length of time with a strong push of water coming down for three or four weeks, then the period immediately after the normal level is reached will often see the pike start to feed ravenously. Back in January 1967 Ray was fishing a water that had been running high and coloured for six whole weeks, during which time the going had been rough. By the middle of the month the water fell rapidly away to normal level and immediately he was into a pike of 20½ lb taken on livebait. Only a mere starter this, however, for over the following fortnight or so that stretch of water really produced the goods. Eleven fish over the 20 lb mark were taken and scores at lesser weights by a mere half-a-dozen anglers.

Such swims, which the pike stick to through thick and thin, may be truly described as pike lairs, and we have tried to distinguish at various places in this book between the methods needed to catch 'easy' pike, that is, when they are *beginning* a big feeding spree, in their lairs, and methods needed to catch 'lazy' pike. Free-line livebaiting, ledgered livebaiting, and sparsely hooked static deadbaits are methods which succeed when things are dour, although they are perfectly good techniques even when the pike are moving well. However, as I implied at the beginning of the chapter, there are less spectacular kinds of lairs occupied by one or more fish more or less permanently.

Newport Long Pond is a water in which we knew the details of the whole of the fishable bank. Good pike swims were marked down, usually where the shallows sloped off quickly into relatively deep water and yet had fringing common reeds. One or two good pike were resident in the swims and one little 6-pounder was a regular to our landing net. It is in these swims, the pike's lairs, that the pike anglers get those takes where the pike swallows the bait without moving. Several waters of my experience, Hornsea and Newport included, had these swallowing-on-the-spot pike long before they had seen many herrings.

If the piker is unfortunate enough to get a pike swallow his hooks badly, and it is impossible to snip the hook to pieces, he should leave the hook in the fish and not attempt any tugging or pulling. That a pike can live with a hook in it is indicated by the numbers of fish I have seen caught with anything up to four sets of trebles in their throats. Judging by the amount of monofil hanging out of their mouths these pike had won the battle in the manner most humiliating for the angler, namely, by snapping him. Bill Chillingworth, Laurie Manns and I once fished a water where *one in four* of the fish caught had hooks and nylon in their mouths. On the other hand Ray and I found a 17½-pounder apparently killed by a huge treble hook in its throat. This fish had also broken its would-be captor, but I must say I have never before or since seen a treble hook as big as that one. To the serious angler, always attentive and thinking about his tackle, I do not think deep hooking remains a problem. Nor do I think stationary deadbait as a method should be banned because it can be abused by the thoughtless. Whilst on the subject of deep hooking I would mention Dug Taylor's suggestion that would solve all problems. Dug thought of putting a single treble hook three inches up the trace above the deadbait's tail (presaging the modern hair rig method).

There is one final hooking arrangement that I should like to mention, and this is the system used by Bill Giles, the renowned Norfolk pike specialist. One leading angling writer described it as all wrong, but since Bill has had over thirty 20 lb pike to this rig it cannot be all that wrong. It has been used with success in many waters, including hotspots (where I myself would not expect it to be very good when the fish were 'off'), and consists of two or three largish trebles tied to thick, single-strand

Preparing minced fish ground-bait balls for the freezer.

Alasticum wire. The herring is attached *facing the wrong way* according
to the traditional methods, but the important point is that on the
retrieve the deadbait comes in head first. Bill takes full advantage of
this on the retrieve and really works it in carefully, and has, in fact,
taken many big pike by doing this. As I say, there cannot be much
wrong with a method used by one of the most successful pike anglers
in Britain. He had his 57th birthday when out with us, and you can
well imagine the years of experience and success that go to make up
his present angling approach. Bill, in fact, was catching pike on herrings
from Broadland hotspots when several famous anglers were saying that
pike on the Broads would not take ledgered deadbaits.

Some strange things happen in hotspots. If you are unlucky enough
to get snapped up you may find the pike reluctant to leave the company
of its fellows. I had two very fluky captures under just such
circumstances, having snapped on the strike when using a large perch
as livebait. The line actually parted just on the stop knot so I must have
pulled it a bit tight. After towing my float about for some time it
decided, seemingly reluctantly, to leave the area and went off way over
to the other side where it holed up close to the bank. Nothing much
was happening so I reeled in to the bank my other rod which was baited
with herring, fitted up a spinning rod, and set off on the half-mile walk
in an attempt to tangle the spinner in the line being pulled around by
the pike. When I finally arrived at the opposite point I found to my
dismay that the 'lost' pike had gone back to the hotspot! At this point
I began to think that fate had it in for me since although my deadbait
rod had been reeled right in to the rod, the 'lost' pike swam round the
deadbait line and began towing it across the water roughly in my
direction. I waited and waited and sure enough in it came to the point
it had visited on its first long wander. Eventually I was able to snag the
lines with the spinner and began playing the fish very, very gently.
Suddenly its strength increased enormously and I found myself playing
two pike; the herring, which was being dragged along by the 'lost' pike,
had itself been taken by a big fish. As I got them both closer to the bank
the first fish managed to slide the line off the spinner, but I played in
the 'herring' fish, and netted it shortly after at 17¾ lb. As 'jammy' a
fish as you could ask for. I went after the first fish again, tangled the
line with the spinner, just below the float, and Mick Griffiths finally
netted it for me at 14½ lb. An angler cannot ask for much more than
that in a day's fishing, yet I reckon I earned my luck. Anyway I got
three more doubles that day.

And then we had the hobnail boot marks. This used to happen on the Hornsea Mere hotspot. No sign of a run and yet when the herring was drawn in it would have some squarish, or rectangular, dents just as though somebody wearing hobnail boots had stamped on it. This happened three or four times, and we never did solve it, but I like to think that my father, a non-angler, came up with the best answer: 'Nay lad, it's a pike so old and so big, that his teeth have been worn down to mere stumps.'

The questions remain, despite all this discourse on hotspots. I cannot really explain them except in terms of the analogy with other predators such as lions. Such an analogy may be quite correct, of course. The last question is how on earth do you find them if they have no certain physical features? It really is a question of trial and error, a matter of drawing together every single thing you know about a water and the fish it has yielded to you and other anglers. Then you have to get down to trying different swims. This can be done with a few friends providing you don't mind sharing fairly when you hit the jackpot. Very careful and laborious spinning with big spoons and plugs might give enough clues to make you put up the bait rods. On long drains you can try the leap-frogging method of fishing, whereby you move on past your companion every half hour or so. The main drawback here is that you may go right through a hotspot *outside* the feeding period and all is wasted. I do know several waters where I have never found a hotspot. But that experience should never lead you to think that they are a figment of my imagination. I once began to feel like that on a water, and then someone else found it . . .

CHAPTER TWELVE

King pike

Some might argue that the salmon is the king of freshwater, but the salmon is largely in the rivers, and even then only at intervals – and when there he doesn't eat! No, the pike is king of the freshwater ecological pyramid at the present, and even if carp and catfish locally eclipse him on grounds of weight it is the pike that sits atop the food chain. His only danger today comes from humans, and it is partly that danger I wish to discuss in this chapter.

But firstly I want to consider the rôle of the pike in the past, and in what I'll term for the moment, natural fisheries. The pike has been around for at least thirty million years, that is some six times as long as we humans, and in all that time he has cleared the waters of neither roach nor trout. There are good reasons why not. No predator removes his supply of food; there is an ever shifting balance between too much pressure on the prey or too much pressure on the predator. For example, in a water where too great inroads are made into, say, the roach stocks, then the pike will start to eat other species *including their own offspring*. By this means the number of predators reaching maturity declines and the stock of roach builds up again. Pike, in fact, have a strong tendency to keep their own offspring in control either by eating them or by confining them to small niches on a water, such as thick weed beds or shallows. Only when the water cools can jack pike spread around more freely because the big pike feed less often and less heavily.

It could be said that there is no such thing today as a natural fishery, that man has altered all. By and large I can accept this argument, but there are exceptions in the wilder parts of the world, even in these islands of ours, as well as in waters *that have lain fallow* for a decade or so. I have at intervals fished such waters and the ecology is revealing and, I think, reflects the fishy world before man came along and messed it up. Several features stand out. In the first place the other fishing, be it roach, tench, or what have you, tends to be good. And the pike are not much in evidence. Indeed, on quite a number of waters the club leasing the waters at a later stage were quite unaware of the presence of pike. I know one water with big pike where the club running it are quite ignorant of the fact, and have been so for at least fifteen years!

Such waters are not uncommon. Jack pike are conspicuous by their absence. In truth they *are* there but you have to look for them, for they spend most of their time in the middle of weed beds or in inaccessible, weedy shallows and you can best find them by climbing trees. The big pike are present and usually they are located, for much of the time, in quite small areas of the lake. Unless someone flukes a jack pike or, with luck, a big pike (as when someone, ignorant of the fact that there *are* no pike, actually fishes for them!) they can remain quiet for years. An experienced piker can get quite good, peaceful piking on waters like this if he behaves in a sensibly circumspect fashion.

The problem arises when the pike are discovered by all. You can imagine their reaction: 'Someone has put pike in our lake'. Alternatively, the pike will take a hammering from pike anglers themselves as the word gets out. So whether it is bad handling by pikers, or culls run by the club in charge, big pike become scarcer as they are

The scale from a pike whose length was 38½″, girth, 22″, and weight, 20 lb. Note that the rings are *relatively* easy to read, though this is not always the case.

removed or are killed (or both). Once this happens the resulting progress of the lake follows an inexorable pattern:

1. The number of jack pike caught increases because with the main danger to them removed they come out of the weed beds and hunt more widely. (As I have put it before, remove the chiefs and the indians run amok.)

2. For the same reason pike manage to overbreed so you get more jacks added to the original head of jacks.

3. Before long the jacks begin to interfere with roach fisherman, and match anglers, and the cry goes up that the lake is overpopulated with jacks, which it is, of course.

4. Culls then take place and as many pike as possible are removed by the club. In fact this does no good at all because every couple of years or so it is clear that there are still too many jacks present. Repeated culls simply keep the jack pot on the boil.

This rotten carcass was one of many found by a Cumbrian reservoir in 1980. Happily, such a sight is now becoming rare as anglers increasingly appreciate the natural role of pike in water.

The answer, of course, is to put in big pike in small numbers, say one big double-figure fish per acre. But try telling that to a club! It is, however, the road back to reducing the jack population and the total biomass of pike (because any water is able to sustain a bigger biomass of pike if the pike are small; the predation on roach is then greater). All this has been known for at least a couple of decades. There is scientific work, as on Lake Windermere; there is fisheries management work, as in the numerous Irish waters; there are specialist anglers' observations; there is evidence from coarse fisheries, small and large;

there is even unambiguous evidence from trout waters. But still the ignorant go on culling pike in a futile attempt to cut their numbers: they are, in actual fact, *increasing* their numbers and decreasing their average size; and increasing the predation! What a world. Why don't we go back to nature, to what we know works, and enjoy our fishing again? After all, who wants waters teeming with jacks? The match-men? The pleasure anglers? The pike anglers? No one does.

The pike's rôle then is as king, a controller of populations, and it is to the pike's advantage to have a good head of fodder fish. This is the way things evolved through time and it is up to us to allow as natural a situation as possible. It is in all our interests as anglers, whatever our particular discipline. Do mark my words, because in about twenty-five years on my estimate we'll be doing what I am suggesting. It will take the trout managers that long to realise.

Let me just enlarge a little on that last statement. There is at present a feeling that trout are needed to grow big, giant, fat pike. This is wrong. As I write there have been two 40-pounders from the Norfolk Broads, and one previously, and certainly at least two of those came from waters with hardly any trout in them. It is also said that pike grow big and fat in trout waters, such as Grafham, because they eat the trout. I'm sure they do eat trout, especially unhealthy rainbows, but the only reason the pike feast on trout in Grafham is because the authorities *remove the coarse fish* upon which pike more easily feed. They also feed more selectively on coarse fish when the latter are present in vast quantities, e.g. perch on Windermere. Pike have more difficulty catching healthy trout and, to take Windermere again as an example, the only times that lake's char and trout became at risk was when the perch in Windermere were removed or suffered perch disease. This proves conclusively that the pike prefer the easier to catch and more numerous perch. Therefore, if you wish to have giant pike in a trout water, remove your coarse fish, but forget then about your trout fishing unless you have more money than sense with which to stock *ad infinitum*.

Some of these remarks may strike some readers as heretical, but it is worth recording that when, a number of years ago, people claimed pike were scavengers they were laughed at. There is still a great deal to learn about pike, and one of the real hindrances to progress has been the quite ludicrous legends of history that portray the pike not as king but as a baddy, a killer. It plays a vital rôle in the ecology of most waters.

CHAPTER THIRTEEN

Pike Angler's Club of Great Britain

Angling surveys have shown on more than one occasion that pike are Britain's second most popular quarry, second only to roach. In view of the pike's opinion of roach he probably shares that sentiment entirely, and he may equally be aware that humans find *him* a desirable capture! Such surveys need to be treated with some caution because if one asks 'Do you ever/occasionally/regularly/often fish for – ?' the answer with roach and pike is that you'll find a tick somewhere along the line simply because the majority of anglers were brought up with these two fish: roach first, pike shortly afterwards – as they became aware how their roach catches were being attacked. Nevertheless, stemming from this very beginning, roach and pike have always been treated differently: the roach as a goody; the pike as a baddy. The contrast could not be sharper. One used delicate tactics for roach whereas piking was concerned with crude tackle, some noise, and equally crude excitement. Over the last century countless first-class pike waters have been destroyed as pike have been indiscriminately slaughtered – the result, as I explained in Chapter Twelve, is waters full of tiddly pike which are a thundering nuisance to everyone.

Despite the great interest in pike it is surprising that a specialist club wasn't founded much earlier than it was. The Fly Fishers' Club was founded in the last century and many game fishermen did a deal of pike angling too. I suppose that because they operated under the gross and distorted image of the rôle of pike in nature they saw no need for a club. Their 'interest' wasn't that deep. Pike were only put there by God to *be* slaughtered. Indeed, the vast increase in knowledge of piking techniques since 1960 shows quite clearly that their interest wasn't that deep. Even so, with men like Bickerdyke and Jardine around, one cannot but help but wonder . . .

The Pike Society

It was inevitable that with the new post-war awareness of angling, and the general penchant at the time for founding clubs and societies, a Pike Society would be formed. I remember well its hesitant beginnings, and also its demise. Quite who had the idea for a national society isn't clear; it may have been Fred Buller, or Richard Walker or Eric Hodgson. In any event some of us in the Cambridge region were consulted very early on, and a meeting was actually held, in 1971, at the White Horse pub in Milton, my own village. The aim of the meeting seemed to be two-fold; Fred Buller and Richard Walker spent some time trying to persuade us all to conquer the pike of Loch Lomond (and none of us were interested because we were getting better fish elsewhere!); and, secondly, there were a few quiet soundings about the formation of a national pike society. I cannot recall all the anglers present but I do remember, in addition to those mentioned already, Ray Webb, Bill Giles, Reg Sandys, Jim Gibbinson and Hugh Reynolds. Not many months later a meeting took place at Melton Mowbray, which I recall being attended by at least fifty anglers, including most of the famous pike anglers of the day such as Wagstaffe and Reynolds, Clive Loveland, Mike Prorok as well as most of those from the Milton meeting.

I recall too that there was a certain amount of debate about two basic ways of running the show: one was the Wagstaffe/Reynolds way in which the club would be totally open to anyone who wanted to fish for pike; the second was that the club should be élitist and rather small, not much more than the size of the Melton Mowbray gathering. At the end of the day the Wagstaffe/Reynolds feeling marginally won, and within a few short years the club, the Pike Society, was virtually dead, and only in one year did the membership exceed 100. That was in its second year I think; the third year it dropped to 70; and thereafter it declined steadily.

I deliberately linked the decision and the result above because I believe they *were* linked. The first meetings of the society were keenly attended by experienced pikers, but subsequently these dwindled and most meetings were attended by newcomers seeking knowledge. Most of the old hands, naturally, didn't want to impart it or were incapable of doing so. With the really experienced anglers simply not bothering to rejoin, the society was doomed and both the first President, Fred Buller, and the second, myself, were disappointed if not too surprised. I think we had both favoured an élitist organisation that would lead the way, inspire, and eventually change the face of pike angling. In the event I think the piking fanatics did that, by their writings, and helped not a little, we like to think, by *Fishing for Big Pike*.

John Watson with a 30 lb 2 oz fish from Norfolk's river Thurne.

Birth of P.A.C.

As the society neared death in 1977, Eric Hodgson, saviour of so many angling causes, got in touch with Hugh Reynolds and I and asked us if we'd take over the club, not as figureheads but actually running it. We hesitated for some time. Forming a new society is rather different from resuscitating a dying duck. For a start, people would be suspicious of the old club because it *had* failed. We were also very busy professional men, Hugh with his architecture and myself with geology, our angling being fitted in when it could be. Eventually we decided to go ahead, provided the remnants of the club would give us that go ahead on on our terms. We met Eric Hodgson at a café on the A1 halfway between Sheffield and Cambridge and put our terms to him: a completely free hand to execute all decisions without consultation with a committee; the President, Secretary, and Treasurer to be in the Cambridge area; whilst *we* would be elected by the few paid up members of the Pike Society (fifteen in 1977), we would pick our own President (we had in mind Bill Chillingworth and he later agreed, reluctantly and with some modesty); thereafter we'd make all the decisions, do all the work, but without the *need* to consult. (Of course, we often *did* consult other members, indeed at times made almost a fetish of doing so.)

A meeting of the Pike Society was arranged at Bourne, Lincolnshire on September 11th 1977, and at this meeting we presented our terms to the six members who were able to make it. To our surprise they agreed unanimously, as indeed had some of those unable to attend but who had been contacted by 'phone by Eric Hodgson. Not a single voice was raised in opposition, so we were lumbered! There had been just one minor scare. Hugh and I had insisted that only fully paid up members would be invited to the extraordinary general meeting, but to our horror Eric sent the invitation to all those defunct members of recent seasons. As it happened none of them came!

Four years later, when we handed over what had become known as our benevolent dictatorship to our Norwich replacements, there were about 1400 members, finances were sound, and the club was being listened to nationally and was taking part actively in national and local club activities. The success was due to a series of simple decisions resulting from lessons learned the hard way in the Pike Society. We decided that the club needed a hardcore of experienced anglers upon whom we could call for help and advice, but to keep them we had to protect them and their fishing from the pressure of beginners – enthusiastic, innocent pressure though that was.

We decided on a two-tier system, a category of Senior Members and one of Associate Members, for the experienced and inexperienced respectively. The SMs, as they were called, paid more, were entitled to a copy of the magazine, but were not required to get heavily involved unless they wished to do so. It was a good formula because it worked. The AMs were organised into Regional Associations, actually based upon *centres* rather than areas (i.e. towns!), and each had a Regional Organiser who provided copies of the magazine on a rotary basis. It should be remembered that at that time we were working on a bit of a shoestring and only in phase 2 of P.A.C., when the team from Norwich took over, did the club actually begin to make a sizeable profit and the magazine became a more or less quarterly, glossy production of much higher standard than the cyclo-styled magazine that Hugh and I put together.

At this time, too, the different categories of membership were abandoned, probably correctly because the club was now big enough for any individual member to be as amorphous as he wished to be. For several years the Regional Associations, scattered all over the U.K., have numbered over ninety; the club as a whole has been increasingly active in both local and national activities, and is a member of the N.A.C., N.F.A., A.C.A. and N.A.S.A. I think when Hugh and I attend meetings now we are sometimes a little staggered at how the club took off. Of course there is quite a turnover of members, because as newcomers learn the ropes they inevitably go through a phase of thinking they know it all and they leave. They do eventually return, often at a time when they become mature and feel like putting something back into the sport.

After our own dictatorship there followed one with Vic Bellars as President, John Watson as Secretary and Martyn Page as Treasurer. More recently (1985) the dictatorship has moved to the northwest of England, except for the President, who is Martin Gay of Essex. Malcolm Bannister is Secretary, in Southport and Geoff Parkinson of Lancaster the Treasurer. The replacement dictatorship does work, and will work, provided no group continues for more than three or four years. So far they've been glad to hand over the reins after such a period because the system, which has proved practical, involves a deal of hard work – which cannot be delegated to a committee member! On the other hand the work does get done and P.A.C. is now better than ever and is financially very sound. Ultimately I suppose we'll become properly democratic, but it will be a sad day.

The objectives of the club have always been fairly straightforward: a new deal for the pike and pike anglers; and the dissemination of information to pike anglers to help them improve both their sport and their behaviour. It was always intended that the club would have a good social atmosphere both at local, R.A. level and at the national level. Many local gatherings are held each year, probably about a thousand or so, and at national level there has often been a Christmas Social or similar event and a Regional Organisers Working Dinner is held each year (which any member can attend!).

It is not my intention to dwell on the varied activities and issues with which the P.A.C. has been involved, but suffice it to say that these are covered in detail in issues of the magazine and anyone can join! It is often assumed that the experienced angler learns nothing through P.A.C., that he only contributes. Nothing could be further from the truth. I cannot record, even in this tome of mine, all that I have learned since 1977 through personal contact with many other pikers. This feeling is becoming widespread now, and the equivalents of P.A.C. have been formed in Ireland and in Holland, whilst quite a few of its policies and ideas have taken off in the U.S.A.

I can think of only one sphere where I would consider that P.A.C. has partially failed, and that is in attracting to its ranks the many older anglers who fish for pike. This *may* be because young people tend to be attracted to a club which does, after all, teach very effectively. Older anglers are settled in their ways and are, possibly, quite happy with their piking. However, it is at the moment very noticeable that some older anglers are less successful, not really competent at handling pike, and really could do with a few lessons! There are many reasons why they should join, but none better than to put a little back into the sport they have enjoyed so long. Be all this as it may, P.A.C. is on its way, is becoming a listened-to power in the land, and will ultimately get a clearer recognition of the rôle of the pike in freshwater ecology. To join, you need only to write to Malcolm Bannister, 7 Sunny Road, Southport, Lancs. enclosing a stamped, addressed envelope.

Join the crusade!

Index

Gay, Martin, 17, 28, 34, 140
Gibbinson, Jim, 44, 137
Giles, Bill, 19, 31, 129, 137
Glucose Lake, Rawcliffe Bridge, 31
Grafham Water, 135
Great Ouse, River, 26, 32, 36, 46, 49, 117, 118
Griffiths, Mick, 111
groundbait, 129
gurnard, 35

haddock, 35
Half-baits, 28
Hatherley, Ray, 22
Hempholme lock, 23
herring, 27
Hickling, 16
Higgins, George, 92, 93
HNV, 39
Hodgson, Eric, 137, 139
Hornsea Mere, 16, 26, 27, 48, 107, 126, 128, 131
Horsey Mere, 16
hotspot, 122, 123, 125
Housden, Jim, 84
Hull, River, 23

In-Fisherman, 112

Jardine, Alfred, 54, 137

lairs, pike, 48
landbeach lakes, 109
ledger, swan shot, 46
lines, 66, 75
Livebait, 49; free-line, 46; ledgered, 44; liphooked, 44; paternoster, 51; trolled, 58
location of pike, 116, 121-3
Loch Lomond, 40, 81, 94
Lough Ree, 107, 126
Loveland, Clive, 137
lure bags, 67
lure boxes, 67

mackerel, 27, 38
Manns, Laurie, 15, 32, 118, 125, 129
Market Weighton Canal, 45
Marlinstrand, 40
Merrit, Ernest, 127
Mitchel, 71
Mucilin, 51

N.A.C., 75, 140
National Association of Specimen Groups (N.A.S.A.), 21, 140
netting pike, 99, 100
Neville, John, 16
Newport Long Pond, 24, 27, 119, 128
N.F.A., 140
night feeding, 109
Norfolk Broads, 90, 113, 135
Northern Irish Pike Society, 93

octopus, 36
O'Donnell, Mac, 43
offal, 38
Oliver's of Knebworth, 71
Optonics, 40
oxygen, 114

Page, Martyn, 140
Parkinson, Geoff, 140
Partridge, 40, 75
paternoster, 55-7
P.D.Q., 66
pH, 112, 114
Pike Angler's Club of Great Britain, 9, 58, 104, 136, 139
pike lairs, 48
pike-perch, 26
Pike Society, 137
playing pike, 99
pre-baiting, 27, 38, 129
P.V.A., 76, 80
Pye, Dennis, 54, 56, 86

radio control, 84
Ranby, Bob, 91